The Pilgrim's Companion

The Pilgrim's Companion

A HANDBOOK
FOR THE SPIRITUAL PATH

F. Aster Barnwell

ELEMENT
Shaftesbury, Dorset • Rockport, Massachusetts
Brisbane, Queensland

© 1992 F. Aster Barnwell

Published in the U.S.A. in 1992 by
Element, Inc.
42 Broadway, Rockport, MA 01966

Published in Great Britain in 1992 by
Element Books Limited
Longmead, Shaftesbury, Dorset

Published in Australia by
Element Books Ltd for
Jacaranda Wiley Ltd
33 Park Road, Milton,
Brisbane, 4064

Cover illustration by Kate Elkin
Cover design by Max Fairbrother
Designed by Roger Lightfoot
Typeset by Photoprint, Torquay, Devon
Printed and bound in the U.S.A. by
Edwards Brothers, Inc.

Library of Congress Catalog Card Number available

British Library Cataloguing-in-Publication
Data available

ISBN 1-85230-342-5

To Lisa, Alex, Hanif, Tricia
and their generation

Contents

Preface

This book, *The Pilgrim's Companion,* is a sharing of my heart and life. It testifies to many of the fruits of my own spiritual journey and my ongoing quest to uncover, live, and embody the Complete Truth of my existence. I trust that it also bears witness to that larger and more authentic life that awaits anyone who, with diligence and patience, attempts to incarnate his or her ideals and visions of a spiritual orientation to life. I also hope that the insights I am sharing in these pages will inspire you: first, to awaken more deeply to your own higher possibilities, and second, to take the steps necessary to make them part of your everyday reality.

In reading this book, you will probably discover that it has a life and energy all its own. There is an organic unity in the way that it progresses from the first chapter to the last, building energy as it does so. Even while it was being written, I felt impelled to ensure that my words and expressions came as close as possible to the intuitions and feelings I wanted to express. The result is that I revised it several times, each occasion bringing it closer to its potential. Eventually I was satisfied enough not to want to change anything. Several readings confirmed that it had achieved its completion. For this reason I encourage you not to skip chapters, but to read sequentially. This way, the energy of the book will carry you in its updraft, in a manner of speaking.

The appendix was developed to establish a bridge between the spheres of *seeing* and *being,* the conceptual and the practical. After a first reading of the main body of the book I would encourage you to work through the appendix, doing the various exercises contained in it. This will help you integrate the many insights derived from the book into your personal life. The appendix functions as a step-down transformer, enabling you to channel the awakened energy and inspiration into the practical, everyday arena.

It is my hope that this book will become a true *companion* to you on your journey and be the kind of book you will refer to occasionally even after a complete reading. Also, you may want to work more deeply with the themes in each chapter from time to time. To this end, you will find the glossary useful as a reminder of some of the key ideas and concepts dealt with in various chapters.

Acknowledgments

I gratefully acknowledge the support of the following persons:

- **Peter Roche de Coppens**, for his love, friendship, and for his support of my work. I am particularly grateful for the efforts he has expended in getting my works published in both French and English.

- The following members of my immediate family: **Vernis, Joy, Emelius, and Shirley Barnwell** for supporting me in diverse and significant ways in my single-parenting role as I lived and penned the words of this book.

- **Susan Griffin**, for offering valuable suggestions for improving certain sections of the final draft.

I also gratefully acknowledge all those, seen and unseen, who have crossed my path and have intentionally or unintentionally contributed to my unfolding.

Introduction: A Holistic Perspective on the Transformation of Consciousness

THE PATH OF PROCESS

Like one envelope within another, another Reality comprising a different state of consciousness waits in our collective future. This Reality, though more developed than anything we can imagine, is not yet complete. To complete itself, it has to be anchored in a material setting, and for this, it requires the freewill effort of every one of us. It is up to each of us to make contact with it and embody it by hosting it within ourselves. Through our joint effort, we will create a change in our human nature, and with it, a permanently changed collective human reality.

When I speak of the transformation of consciousness, I envision each one of us playing host to this Higher-Consciousness-Reality and giving it the opportunity to transform our human nature. My perspective differs from many other transformational models currently in vogue in that it sees transformation as a complex endeavor consisting of a triple activity. First, we must contact this Higher-Consciousness-Reality; second, we must host it in our thoughts and aspirations; and third, we must simultaneously give our attention and encouragement to the new nature that the Higher-Consciousness-Reality wants to birth in us.

Because this joint interchange leads to a complex network of psychological interactions, the transformation of consciousness is best understood as a path of process. Seeing it as a path of process prepares us to deal with the multifaceted nature of transformation and the perplexing dilemmas that beset us on our spiritual search. If we accept a narrower perspective on the transformational process, we might not be prepared or equipped to deal with the dilemmas that we must resolve when we enter the spiritual path.

DILEMMAS ON THE TRANSFORMATIONAL PATH

One of the first dilemmas that we encounter on this path emerges from the nature of the transformational pursuit itself. The transformational journey requires the spiritual seeker to enter a process to arrive at the end different from the person who started out at the beginning. Though at the outset we do not know "what we will be," we must organize our energies to propel ourselves toward another state of being and another consciousness that we know little about.

At its beginning, the task before us is equivalent to that of a blind man searching for a black cat in the dark. We are faced with a situation where we must rely on our present, limited perception to define and settle upon a distant objective toward which we must dedicate our life. We are confronted with the need to "do something" without even the assurance that we have the required information to make a proper diagnosis of the situation to be remedied. This insight comes about after a certain degree of spiritual maturity, but is only acquired after our search is well under way.

At the end of the transformative journey we also find a dilemma: upon arriving in a new state of being and consciousness, we find it difficult to chart a path for others to follow. As we look back to assess how we arrived, we see that no specific thing that we have done has precipitated our Realization. In a sense we see that the Realization revealed itself to us by degrees, causing us to empty ourselves through our personal efforts. In the state of Realization, we see our striving as nothing more than a catharsis that created a state of receptivity to a new consciousness.

THE TRANSFORMATIONAL IMPULSE

Though the many dilemmas we face at the outset make for a difficult beginning, our situation, just as that of the blind man, is not as hopeless as it first seems. The blind man knows that the cat exists, and presumably that is why he is searching for it. And should he chance upon it, he has all that is necessary to detect it: his sense of touch. Similarly, the situation of the spiritual seeker would be hopeless were it not for the existence of the transformational impulse. This impulse is a point of contact between each of us and the New-Consciousness-Reality of our collective future. It is a seed of this Reality, existing in each of us — making it possible for us to begin a spiritual search and undertake the journey of transformation.

In a psychological sense, an impulse may be described as a need that is felt at a very deep level of being, a level that lies beneath the reach of rational analysis. Because it exists at such a deep level, it might lie undetected and undifferentiated from other needs in our consciousness. The need that the transformational impulse represents is a yearning for release, a yearning to exceed the confines of our historical selves and to find a larger context for our deepening perception of Life. In more familiar terms, the transformational impulse is humanity's thirst for meaning in life. But this is more than meaning in the sense of a rational explanation to life. It is meaning as a sense of coherence and purpose.

At a superficial level, this thirst for meaning does not appear to have a rational cause, just as there is no rational reason for a plant to produce seeds. Yet in the larger context of the cooperative network of systems that sustain life on the earth, plants have a good reason to produce seeds. By the same token, there is every logical reason for a human being to yearn to find herself in a context larger than her individual existence. If we do not respond to the challenge to seek out and find new identities in ever-widening circles, we may continually bump and bruise ourselves against the limits within which we insist on viewing and relating to Life. The transformational impulse can be considered as an insurance premium that Life pays to ensure that we strive to broaden the context of our existence. It is equivalent to the seed a plant produces.

NAVIGATING THE PATH OF PROCESS

The path to a transformed consciousness is not linear. Traveling this path is not a simple matter of setting up a target and going after it. A linear approach breaks down because it presupposes that what completes the journey is what starts it. But this is certainly not so. Usually it is the ego that starts out on the transformational journey, but for the journey to end in spiritual realization, the ego must be subordinated to something else. Because the transformational path is nonlinear, we must view it as a path of process.

The only way for us to participate successfully in our own transformation is to simultaneously engage in and oversee the process that brings about a metamorphosis of the ego-centered self. We achieve this when we feed the transformational impulse by taking the time and effort to satisfy the inner need to find meaning in life. Such an activity is similar to that of feeding fuel to a fire. In this case, we are both the fire that is fed and the feeder. The fire is fueled by those aspects of ourselves that we outgrow as we achieve clarity on how to seek greater meaning in life, and as we grasp a more stable vision of our collective New-Consciousness-Reality.

The parts of ourselves that we sacrifice into the transformational fire fall into familiar categories: the egotistical designs we have upon Life, petty ambitions, fears, disappointments, shortsighted ideas of success, our sense of alienation, and our separative tendencies. The glow that emanates from this fire reveals our growing sense of meaning and belonging, the wholeness of creation, the oneness of the Creator and the created, the unity of the seeker and that which is sought, and the common identity of the One and the many. Progressively we bring new aspects of our future into manifestation and anchor them in our daily life. This is the key to our transformation, and this is how we change our experience of Life!

We navigate the path of process by placing our attention and sympathy on the process at work within us that propels us toward greater meaning. Our emphasis is not on acquiring anything, but on doing what is necessary to allow right relationships to emerge between the various facets of our selves and the external universe. We make progress by always being open and receptive to the Highest Good that can be perceived in any situation or relationship. Concurrently, we must behave in a manner that is compatible with the Highest Good as we intuit it on an ongoing basis.

Each time we defer to the Highest Good that we can perceive in our encounters and relationships, we achieve a new understanding of our relationship to everything else. Each time such a new understanding occurs, we succeed in transforming ourselves a bit more. In this sense, being consciously on the path of process allows us to reconcile the outer with the inner life. It is also the method which unites effort and Grace and resolves the many dilemmas of the transformational journey.

A PERSONAL RETROSPECTIVE

In many respects I became aware of the transformational impulse in my own life since early adulthood. From the period of my late teens until age thirty, I became aware of an aspiration within me that was unlike any other I held. It occupied a very deep and private place in me and was instrumental in shaping my sense of the purpose of my life and my idea of happiness. Whenever I took time for philosophical reflection, this aspiration would rise to the surface. I would then imagine a time in my life when, like the legendary Adam, I would "walk and talk with God." On a practical level, this dream signified a time when I would feel no barrier between my consciousness and unconstrained Being. I anticipated a time when I would no longer feel like an outsider in my relationship with Life, no longer feel the need to adopt a defensive attitude to life and its vicissitudes. Although I occasionally took refuse in this aspiration, I was content to let it reside in the deepest recesses of my being, where I expected it to hibernate until I had fulfilled my career ambitions and family responsibilities.

However, it turned out that Life had other plans for me. At those times when I gave attention to this aspiration, I was unconsciously invoking the possibility of incarnating a higher consciousness. Moreover, my contemplation of this aspiration acted as a lightning rod to conduct some of these possibilities into my conscious awareness and outer life. By making this aspiration a part of my waking consciousness I was opening myself up to the responsibility of playing host to a higher consciousness in my outer life.

At about the age of thirty, a situation developed whereby all my plans for my life were overturned, creating the opportunity for me to step into a stage of life I had avoided on account of the demands of ordinary living. As the concerns with which I had insulated myself were stripped away, I came face to face with the realization that, instead of fighting my inner impulse toward a fuller spiritual orientation to life, it was possible to pursue my aspiration of a closer relationship with God now. Within myself, I said, "Yes! Why not?"

As I surrendered more deeply to this new commitment, I experienced a deep sense of relief, as if a burden I had been carrying had suddenly lifted. I saw how constructive it would be to dedicate the rest of my life to the task of eliminating the barriers between me and God — now, while I had the strength, instead of waiting for the end portion of my life when my natural abilities and energy would have waned. I also felt that in eliminating the many years of waiting to cultivate that open and full relationship, I would be filling all the years of my life with essential and meaningful content, instead of using my energy to continue building barriers to be surmounted at some future time.

One of the results of my new values and approach to life was the emergence of particular spiritual experiences that I previously knew nothing about and for which I had to seek explanations. With each new experience, I was forced to find a larger context for the changes within me. I accepted these experiences as assurance that the principles I was pursuing and endeavoring to incorporate into my being were working. These experiences encouraged me to intensify my search for meaning. And as I intensified my search, I was able to refine my understanding of the spiritual principles behind these expressions of life as I saw and experienced them.

When I became aware of the significance that I was being called to live out, I made the conscious decision to cooperate with and facilitate the larger process to which the experiences seemed to invite me. I began to reorganize my life to incorporate the openness and vulnerability to which Life was calling me. This decision to consciously facilitate the transformational process has been the key to the pattern of my life ever since.

Over the past fifteen years I have had to let go of a great deal of my concept of myself, which is not unlike being subject to a progressive death. However, while this progressive death began quite painfully at the outset, it has grown smoother so that I now notice changes only in retrospect. The major change to which I have had to adjust is the growing sense that my personal life is not an end in itself. This realization required many adjustments at both a psychological and a practical level. For one, I have had to withdraw many of the projections I had been making on Life: I had to learn that I am not a playwright penning a script that Life has to support, but rather that Life itself is the script writer, and I am part of that script with my own part to play in a grand, dramatic production involving many other actors besides me.

This process of surrender of the outer life has not been without its compensations in the inner one. I have experienced a deepening sense of connectedness with Life and have realized my dream of no longer feeling like an outsider with respect to the movement and vicissitudes of Life. For truly, I know with all my heart and being that the Universe bodes no ill toward me and the ultimate end of all processes in the Universe is Goodness.

This book sums up some of the key insights I have gained from my own transformational journey. It sets out the objective principles that have contributed to my spiritual understanding and have oriented me in my search for a more meaningful life. Although I have liberally interspersed my discussions of principles with examples of my experiences, I regard the reporting of such experiences as a secondary aspect of this work. I share them solely for illustrative purposes, and as evidence to fellow seekers that sincere and determined seeking will bear fruit, not in terms of specific experiences, but in terms of a better understanding and appreciation of Life and its meaning. In this context, the seeker faces a situation similar to that in the biblical story of Jacob wrestling with the angel. We are told that Jacob took hold of the angel and refused to let go until the angel offered him a blessing. Just as Jacob insisted upon receiving a blessing before he released the angel, the spiritual seeker can wrestle with Life's paradoxes, refusing to give up until they yield whatever power and insight into Reality they possess. There is really nothing mysterious about this, for even in Nature the clouds yield to the mountain and give up whatever moisture they contain.

For me, writing this book has been a meditation spanning several years, and to those who are receptive, I hope it provides practical and usable insights, making unnecessary some of the circuitous wanderings that characterize our experience of the spiritual maturation process.

I   Difficulty at the Beginning

RECOGNIZING THE TRANSFORMATIONAL IMPULSE

At some point in life, we might be confronted with the question of whether there is purpose to our lives as individual human beings, and perhaps whether there is purpose to life in general. This urge to probe the purpose of our existence may be precipitated by a life crisis, one that may leave pain, bereavement, and confusion in its wake. Prior to this time, we may have been in full control of the elements of our life and may even have been considered successful. But now our world is turned topsy-turvy, and, perhaps for the very first time, we are forced to seek out and examine the submerged roots of our personal existence. We find ourselves asking: *Who am I? What am I doing here? Why was I born? What will happen to me when I die?*

Despite this chaos in the outer life, a person at this point is actually quite fortunate. For in actuality, he is becoming a point of emergence for Nature's impulse to become conscious of itself, and is giving this impulse an opportunity to refine itself and speed up its progress. This is accomplished when the transformational impulse receives the cooperation of the human mind. What has hitherto been a slow crawl to consciousness accelerates in quick, purposive strides toward the Source of existence. In effect, disruptions in life present an opportunity for the evolutionary impulse to give way to the transformational impulse.

The transformational impulse is the thirst in humanity for meaningfulness. It springs from a need that is deep and primordial. The transformational impulse supersedes the evolutionary impulse, which is the need for adaptation in order to survive, to belong, to be accepted. When the transformational impulse emerges, we find ourselves embarking upon the most challenging period of life, but nevertheless one that is ultimately the most rewarding, because we are presented with an opportunity to individualize our beings, to seek out the places in the Universe that were created with us specifically in mind.

Since the transformational impulse, or the need for meaning, is not a common pursuit in human affairs, the issue here is whether it will take root and prosper, whether we will lend it our conscious cooperation and provide the proper medium within which it can prosper with longevity. The problem we face is critical; the quest for meaning in life is opposed by the mistaken notion that each personal life is an end unto itself, and that the purpose of life is fulfilled in the pursuit of happiness. When we operate under such illusions, we cannot accommodate the impulse towards meaning-fulness, since we will be preoccupied with the pursuit of sensation.

When an individual faces the opportunity to host the transform-ational impulse, the significance of what is taking place in her life may totally elude her. The transformational impulse is usually born when the illusions surrounding the real purpose of life are shattered. Usually, this occurs at a time of major crisis, and the individual who sees happiness as the *raison d'être* of life may react to the impulse towards meaningfulness as an irritation to be soothed — an itch to be scratched.

We can classify the irritations[1] that foreshadow the emergence of the transformational impulse in several categories. These include physical and emotional pain, mental anguish and depression, a sense of spiritual alienation and displacement, and finally, a feeling of lacking power or control over the course of one's life (e.g., alcoholic addiction).

When negatively interpreted, these irritations might lead us to harden our attitudes and pursue diversions to soothe them or escape from them. But since the pain is really the result of Consciousness in the process of giving birth to itself, we quickly realize that negative behavior does not help; at best it provides only temporary relief. In order to reach the irritation and apply balm, we must penetrate great depths. We must plumb many layers of material that constitute our personality: attitudes, motives, emotions, and assumptions about Reality. We get to know ourselves in the process.

The acknowledgment of the transformational impulse requires the cooperation of will, mind, body, and soul (i.e., aspirations). At this point, we begin to ask questions appropriate to the irritation that we are experiencing most acutely.

We may want to know why physical and emotional pain is happening to us in particular. This enquiry ultimately leads to an examination of our attitudes and approach to life. Those of us who are responding to mental anguish and depression may ask whether life is worth living. Eventually we may explore various philosophical systems for personal answers.

Those of us who are experiencing spiritual alienation and displacement might want to know how we each can find our niches in the Universe — the places we alone can fill. We might culminate this phase of questioning by adopting religious and spiritual disciplines.

Finally, for those of us who are responding to the irritation of a loss of control over the course of our life, the questions that emerge show a willingness to surrender our individual wills to the Will of God. Here we may ask anyone and everyone who we think can help, "What shall I do?" Eventually we may end up in a life of service to humanity.

Other scenarios may not be as clear-cut as the above examples. Some individuals may respond to several difficulties simultaneously, with a spectrum of questions overlapping one another. In such complex cases, the response may be a mixture of seeking self-knowledge, wisdom, understanding, religious transcendence, and unity with the Universal through surrender in service. Whatever the combination, the overall effect is an elevation in the quality and direction of effort in our life as we shift from unconscious to conscious striving. Where previously our striving had its roots in insecurity, it is now based on the quest for meaningfulness.

SIMILARITIES BETWEEN TRANSFORMATION AND HUMAN REPRODUCTION

The circumstances within which the transformational impulse is born in our consciousness are sometimes very desperate. Consequently, the psychological environment within which it makes its appearance is often very hostile to its survival and longevity. Jacob Needleman, in his book *Lost Christianity*, puts the problem in perspective, noting that

> [The soul] is not a fixed entity . . . It is an actual energy, but one that is only at some beginning stage of its development and action. Every day, every more or less average human individual experiences the appearance of this energy in its most embryonic stage . . . But almost always, almost without any exception whatsoever, this new energy is immediately dispersed and comes to nothing. A hundred, a thousand times a day, perhaps, "the soul is aborted."[2]

Dr. Needleman's assessment underscores the point that the average individual misses many opportunities to incubate in consciousness the qualities and values that would eventually lead to the birth of the level of existence we call the Soul.

In the sense that the transformational quest explores how we can incubate, in our consciousness, the seed of our personal and collective transformation, it follows that the terms that best capture the dynamics of this quest at the personal level resemble those we use to describe the biological process of human reproduction. The transformational impulse must be conducted through stages similar to that of the human fetus — conception, gestation, labor, and delivery. To complete the picture in true-to-life detail, we can also add false pregnancy, false labor, and regrettably, spontaneous abortion.

We also find imagery relating to the process of human reproduction used in the book of Revelation to portray the transformational process. In the twelfth chapter of Revelation, the process of transformation is described as ". . . a woman clothed with the sun, and the moon under her feet, and upon her head a crown of twelve stars: And she being with child cried, travailing in birth, and pained to be delivered" (Rev. 12: 1–2).

The representation of the transformational process as a pregnant woman speaks to a deep truth of our existence, namely, in relation to the reality of Spirit we are all feminine and "with child" at various stages of the process. We will also find that the precautions and observances required of the mother-to-be — if the life she is carrying is to be brought to term — are also required of us as we host in our beings the impulse towards meaning.

We should keep this image in mind for future reference. Later on, as we wind up our study of how the transformational impulse resolves itself, we will return to it to see how the Revelation drama of the woman with child is resolved.

THE INGREDIENTS OF CONSCIOUS STRIVING

The level of striving required to enable us to extract meaning out of life involves the cooperation of the inner and outer being. This type of effort is not satisfied simply by the adoption of techniques. If we are to succeed in this quest we must be fully convinced that there is no viable alternative in life than to take the transformational journey; hence, we must be prepared to consecrate all aspects of our being to it. We must deal with inner processes to come to terms with how we perceive and respond to the world. We must learn to distinguish between what is objective and what is projected onto the world.

This rearrangement of our perception allows us to achieve a high degree of coordinated functioning so that inner and outer forces work together to promote greater awareness. The part each of us must play to bring about this realignment of perception is to make three conscious, preferably simultaneous inputs into the process.

A Philosophy of Life

The first of these inputs must be made at the highest level of Being accessible to ordinary consciousness, and it requires us to clarify what it is that we aspire toward. Here we must contemplate the scope and dimension of what Life is and what it requires of us. This input is as basic and necessary as the members of a musical ensemble finding out what the score is before starting a performance. From this vantage point, we must specify the objectives we will strive for in our personal lives. This requirement is satisfied when we are able to develop a philosophy of life.

A Value System

The second input requires that we use the information from the first to enquire into how, in actuality, to make the expression of Life on earth compatible with its Universal design. We need to utilize our imagination to preview how our lives will change in a practical, everyday sense, once we've put our insights into practice. This exercise will protect us from dwelling too much in the world of ideas without due regard for the domain of action. This part of the work is satisfied when we consciously adopt a value system or a system of ethics.

Practical Application

The third input calls for us actively to seek ways to regulate inner processes (attitudes) and conduct our outer being in conformity with our personal understanding of how Life, as a principle, is universally expressed. We might call this input practical application. It preserves the integrity of the spiritual journey by acknowledging the fact that, since we exist in time-space to begin with, we can actualize or bring into concrete expression the three-dimensional embodiment of a level of spiritual aspiration. This movement calls for the incorporation of attitudes that directly affect biopsychic functioning and clear a channel to higher energies. This requirement protects us from the fragmentation that occurs when we treat spiritual life as something removed from practical life without any point of reconciliation.

Meditation

Complementary to these three inputs, there is a need to use our attention constantly to bring the results of synthesis into awareness.

This is meditation, and this activity is the pivotal point of our conscious involvement in the process of transformation.

What we now have is a state wherein the spirit, mind, and body are engaged in a united endeavor. Their point of synthesis is the Soul, and it is the extent to which the Soul is brought into expression that meaning is derived from life. The fruit of this approach is self-knowledge, which includes information on all aspects of our psyche. Thus, we become aware of our motives, repressed emotions, false assumptions, unreasonable expectations, illusions, and also our capacity to cope under stress and crisis. Through this process we discover our capacity to love and to be receptive to wholeness. This knowledge also marks the beginning of spiritual consciousness.

Notes, Chapter 1

1. Irritation is used in the biological sense, which is our capacity to react to external stimuli.
2. Jacob Needleman, *Lost Christianity — A Journey of Rediscovery to the Center of the Christian Experience* (New York: Bantam Books, 1982), 170.

2   Values, Conscience, Will: Building Blocks of Spiritual Consciousness

SPIRITUAL CONSCIOUSNESS

Spiritual consciousness is a quality of being that is sensitive and receptive to the necessity, existence, and beauty of the movement in life toward wholeness. Spiritual consciousness is an expression of cooperativeness and connectedness, and therefore LOVE. It is not sufficient that we only desire spiritual consciousness, for it is not a power in the ordinary sense of the word. We must understand spiritual consciousness as the only meaningful outcome and ultimate ripening of human life. Spiritual consciousness is therefore a logical consummation of the Life principle.

A fundamental feature of the Life principle is its ability to organize greater and greater levels of wholeness. We witness this occurring at the level of the human body, where various cells organize into tissues, which then organize into organs, and then into systems, then into this wonderful complexity of the human body. From this combined effort, we get something that is more than the sum of the parts, such that each cell, tissue, organ, and system can derive a benefit from the whole that on its own could not attain. When we speak of the pursuit of spiritual consciousness, we are speaking of consciously extending this process toward increasing organization and wholeness beyond our separate ego-centered identities.

SUBJECTIVE AND OBJECTIVE VALUES

Each time we make a decision or commit an act, we do so on the basis of our value system. A value system is that which lies behind our motivation to act or not act in a specific way. For most of us, a value system may not be the result of conscious choice, but the result of cultural conditioning, which we then express in terms of personal preferences and societal norms. To the extent that values are based on societal and personal standards, the motivation to act, which emanates from them, is under the influence of egocentricity and ethnocentricity.

Values are critical for transformation since the transformational process requires that we progressively universalize our being. The process of universalization requires that the motivations that lead us to act have a greater good in mind than personal comforts or societal norms. To reach such high levels of motivation, our personal value system must first become universalized or objectified.

In a universal or objective value system, the values become increasingly valid as the number of people who uphold them grows. Objective values reinforce themselves as they are expressed, making it progressively easier for additional individuals to uphold them. This contrasts with egocentric and ethnocentric values, which can lose their validity as the number of people who adopt them grows. The validity of these values diminishes in line with how widely they are observed, because they usually bring into conflict the egocentric and ethnocentric values held by other groups and individuals.

A familiar example of an objective or universal value is the Golden Rule: *Do unto others as you would have them do unto you.* So universal is this value that it is found (in slightly different words) in ten of the major religions around the world: Christianity, Confucianism, Buddhism, Hinduism, Islam, Sikhism, Judaism, Jainism, Zoroastrianism, and Taoism (see illustration).

Objective values facilitate the transformational process by allowing us to make contact with higher levels of reality and to receive insight concerning how to take advantage of opportunities for growth that present themselves from time to time. In this manner, objective values shorten the time and reduce the suffering

THE GOLDEN RULE
In Ten of the World's Great Religions

Christianity:
". . . All things whatsoever ye would that men should do to you, do ye even so to them . . ."

Confucianism:
"Do not unto others what you would not they should do unto you."

Buddhism:
"In five ways should a clansman minister to his friends and familiars — by generosity, courtesy and benevolence, by treating them as he treats himself, and by being as good as his word."

Hinduism:
"Do not to others, which if done to thee, would cause thee pain."

Islam:
"No one of you is a believer until he loves for his brother what he loves for himself."

Sikhism:
"As thou deemest thyself so deem others. Then shalt thou become a partner in heaven."

Judaism:
"What is hurtful to yourself, do not to your fellow man."

Jainism:
"In happiness and suffering, in joy and grief, we should regard all creatures as we regard our own self."

Zoroastrianism:
"That nature only is good when it shall not do unto another whatever is not good for its own self."

Taoism:
"Regard your neighbor's gain as your own gain and regard your neighbor's loss as your own loss."

normally associated with the growth of consciousness at the personal level.

When we live primarily on the basis of subjective values (i.e., values determined on the basis of personal preferences and societal norms), our consciousness grows at the point where we evaluate the consequences that flow from an action and compare it to the motivation that preceded it. If the consequences are pleasant, the motivation that gave rise to the act receives a positive reinforcement. If they are unpleasant, a negative reinforcement is received. At this rate, our possibilities for growth are confined within the context of the values of our society.

Societal values provide acceptance or censure for a very narrow range of behavior, and as such they may lose their relevance outside of the boundaries of a particular community, country, or time period. The type of individual they succeed in creating is of likewise limited "durability." If an individual is removed from one community and placed in another, she may have to learn to conform all over again.

Just as personal and societal values succeed in making our behavior acceptable only within a local context, objective values allow us to broaden our scope, thereby giving us acceptance on a scale that is universal. This is because such values strengthen the mind's capacity for moral and spiritual discernment and thus lay the necessary conditions for the development of will. With the capacities of discernment and will, we become capable of measuring our motives and actions by objective standards and are able to translate ideals and principles into their down-to-earth, everyday applications. If we lack these capacities, conscious participation in the transformational process will be limited to occasions when we evaluate our actions and motives from their consequences.

How Objective Values Sharpen the Mind

The mind in its ordinary mode of operation will experience the adoption of an objective value system as a restriction. But just as a bridle helps a rider control a horse and direct its energy in a particular direction, a system of objective values harnesses the powers of the mind and brings it under the control of levels of being beyond the ego.

When we adopt objective values, they give permanence to our being on a scale proportionate to the scope of the values. For example, if we decide to make the cause of world peace a personal concern, then we will begin to experience a personal burden for the cause of world peace. Every event that promotes peace will be felt as a personal success and every event that sets it back will be felt as a personal setback.

When our personal concerns converge with universal ones, we become attuned with others who hold the cause dear. In effect, through our personal commitment we become unified in a collective cause. This is how we gain "objective existence," which means that our reason for existence becomes validated by the very fact that others are living for the same reason.

Objective values enhance our capacity for moral and spiritual discernment, because they make us more aware of the objective world of others and encourage us to take account of the well-being of others when making plans for our own welfare. It is also to the extent that we take account of others in our personal decisions that we develop conscience. Without conscience, we cannot become contributing members of the world community, since the capacity to feel for the community is lacking. It is through the faculty of conscience that concerns for the community become translated into personal goals and that personal actions are examined against a universal context.

Psychologically speaking, conscience and our adherence to objective values bring about a state of creative tension in the being. This tension arises when we are faced with the choice of an act that departs from our concept of correct behavior. When our conscience is fully developed, it functions as an adjudicator. It assesses our actions and responds with the appropriate feeling, usually of a higher emotional nature.

Such feelings as shame, guilt, and anxiety, on one hand, and courage, peace of mind, and contentment, on the other, are all the results of conscience. Because these feelings exist, we are able to sample the consequence of an action before we act. In this sense we can have advance knowledge of which actions are compatible with our ideal world and which ones depart from it. And since we do not have to experience the consequence of an act before we can evaluate its appropriateness, but can feel into its consequence in advance, the mind's powers of moral and spiritual discernment are exercised and sharpened. With a better equipped mind, we give birth to the faculty of will.

FROM CONSCIENCE TO WILL

In the context of the transformational impulse, will is our capacity to engage voluntarily in actions that facilitate personal growth. As said before, when conscience is present, we are able to take the well-being of others into consideration before we act. It is through such deeds that our own individual transformation is facilitated. This principle asserts that we cannot grow beyond the historical self from an ego-centered perspective (one that is concerned with preserving our self-definition) but only from a higher definition of self. In other words, transformation implies far more than acquiring additional powers; it requires a change in our nature. We must grow from individual units of nature to contributive and nurturing members of the human family. This is how will is developed. It accumulates out of our awareness of the existence of a Greater Whole. In a sense, then, will is the drawing force of this Greater Whole, in very much the same way that the gravitational field of the sun exerts a pull on the earth, and that of the earth exerts a pull on the moon.

In the absence of a well-developed conscience, the will may be stunted, because we lack the motivation to undertake actions that do not promise an immediate reward. With conscience, however, it is sufficient motivation for us to know our actions will be of service to the human community. Conscience also enables us to dedicate ourselves to the collective advancement of the human family and of Nature. In this sense, we regard our own trans-formation not only as personal enrichment, but as a responsibility to the human community. Conscience and will enable us to undertake feats that would not be attempted if the only reasons behind them were personal ones.

The importance of will in the transformational quest cannot be overemphasized, for without it human collective evolution is not possible. The will is a necessary condition for our collective evolutionary advancement. Before a faculty or a principle can become a collective heritage of the species, someone, somewhere, must recognize its importance and give it embodiment and physical birth. Unless this step is taken, new faculties can never be part of our human reality.

This principle of embodiment implies that when each of us struggles with our weaknesses to overcome them, or struggles to embody a higher quality of thinking or way of being, we do so not only for ourselves, but for the rest of humanity as well. It is a division of labor of sorts, the very principle that catapulted parts of the world out of the agricultural into the industrial age. As we stand at the threshold of another cultural epoch, "division of labor" will also be required to bring about the next evolutionary shift.

Replenishing the Transformational Impulse

We have already seen how the faculty of will gives us the ability to sublimate personal needs in support of our collective advancement. Will also furthers the transformational process by helping us acquire the necessary understanding to facilitate transformation at a personal level.

It is common knowledge that before any new understanding can be added to someone's perceptual world, room must be created in the mind for it. We create it through the sense of discomfort that arises from either a psychological or a physiological irritation. It is only when our discomfort leads us to question what we've heretofore taken for granted that our mind becomes receptive to new knowledge.

The capacity of the mind to grow is regulated by the degree to which we are able to generate questions, and that, in turn, by the extent to which we experience irritations. When will is present, we are always asking questions, because we are in a perpetual state of irritation. This does not mean that we are irritable in the ordinary sense (being grouchy), but that we are sensitive to the growing pains of humanity as well as our own and as a result always feel at the edge. When we are committed to transformation as a collective endeavor as much as we are committed on a personal level, we always find issues that generate concerns.

BECOMING OUR OWN TEACHER

The depth of understanding we receive from our spiritual enquiry is directly linked to the quality of the questions we seek answers to. A question has "quality" in relation to the sincerity with which it is asked and the breadth of the concerns that it embraces. For instance, questions concerned with the purpose of life, when asked in all earnestness, would rate with those of the highest quality. Many other philosophical questions, provided they are asked with a genuine humility and a willingness to act on what is received, would also rate as high-quality questions. Provided that we have reached a high level of moral functioning and have gained a degree of objective existence by our personal commitment to universal principles, we are able to acquire further understanding of Life simply by pondering questions relevant to the irritations that we feel.

The key to such autonomous revelations is committing ourselves to a life of principles. When we are so engaged, we do not seek understanding for its sake alone. The kind of understanding we seek is usually related to (a) discovering the implications, for our personal life, of the spiritual principles we've discerned, and (b) uncovering the hidden spiritual purpose behind earthly events. This way, we each become our own teacher and our own counsel, since we will have the wherewithal to continuously challenge and spur ourselves onto newer and newer realizations.

STAYING THE COURSE

After we've engaged the process of conscious striving, we stay on course by taking assurance that the process is engaged and taking effect. This assurance is not obtained through intellectual means, but is inferred from the clarity of conscience and peace of mind that we experience. These states of being are the fruits of conscious striving and will be present even when our life may have all the outward signs of difficulty. If we expect external confirmations that we are on the right path, we may set ourselves up for disappointments, or worse, depression and delusion. We must be satisfied to live in the awareness that, since we have done all within our power to facilitate the transformational process, *All Is Well.* When we achieve this level of poise, there will be no visible difference between this stage of the transformational journey and the end, since we will already be experiencing the states that the transformational process will ultimately culminate in — *peace, harmony, and equanimity.*

PROGRESSIVE PERFECTION

Here is a dilemma arising from the transformational process: Where do we get the energy to stay on course when there is apparently no visible, usable goal to our striving? Before we embarked on the transformational journey, all our endeavors culminated in what we then viewed as personal happiness. But as we progress on the journey we find that the former goals do not suffice, so we begin to shoot for more permanent objectives and find that it is not necessary to strive for anything specific, but only to keep our attention focused on the point of synthesis of the various parts of our being. The energy to sustain us in the quest comes from the pull of higher aspects of the Self.

The energies of the higher aspects of the Self become available to us to the extent we are able to sublimate the ego-centered self. The process of sublimation is experienced as successive changes in our center of awareness: it progressively changes to reflect greater and greater wholes. Each new experience of the center then exerts a gravitational pull on us that is greater than the previous one. This way, we are able to reach beyond our perceived limitations, and we progress in perfection.

In addition to the pull of the higher aspects of the Self, there is a push from other parts of the being. This push occurs as the transition from one level of being to another is accompanied by a loss of power at the previous level. We experience a sense of rudderlessness as the perfection that caps our striving at one level of being becomes inadequate for the next level. Even before the new level is revealed, we may feel obliged to organize all of our efforts to achieve perfection at this next level as well.

As a center of consciousness is robbed of its authority over our being, it becomes submerged into another center. We can draw a parallel between the stages and relationships a man may go through during his life: At first, he is someone's son, and all his activities are organized toward being the perfect son, to bring joy to his parents. However, as he grows, he assumes other relationships, which command more of his energy and attention than pleasing his parents. Although he may not deliberately do anything to cause his parents emotional discomfort, their happiness is not his sole preoccupation. He may marry and become a husband to a woman, and this relationship gives him a larger center to work with, demanding more energy and responsibility. There is a great deal of difference between being the perfect son and the perfect husband, and it is quite clear that the perfection of the former state will not satisfy the norms of perfection of the latter, even though it may set the stage for it. Still further, this individual can become a father, and in his endeavor to be the perfect father he will have to divert some of his energy and attention from his previous relationships. His role as father is originating from a more power-ful center, since he has the power to influence and mold someone else's life. In addition to all these relationships, in an exceptional case, this man may become the leader of a political jurisdiction and will have to make decisions that will affect numerous people.

Each of these relationships has its own norms of perfection, but being perfect at a previous level increases the possibility of attaining perfection at the higher level of functioning. At a higher level of perfection, we have more energy to work with, such that our acts have a greater impact on those around us.

Priming the Pump

During the transformational journey, we undergo several deaths. The self which underwent a voluntary death at the outset, when we changed our orientation from subjective to objective values, gained perfection in aspiration at that time. As this perfection is attained, we discover that this perfection is not sufficient to satisfy our spiritual yearnings born at the submergence of the previous level of identity. The level of being that currently exists also strives for its own perfection and accomplishes this when it undergoes a voluntary death to make way for a higher level of being.

The rebirths which follow these deaths become possible through the process we shall call *shadowing*.[1] This process enables us to prepare for the next level of responsibilities appropriate to a higher level of being, even when we may lack the resources that will be available on the higher level. Thus, shadowing is accompanied by what we can call conscious sacrifice, which in reality is an exchange. Shadowing allows us to function as if a higher level of being was already in charge well before its birth takes place. This principle can also be called *priming the pump*.

Notes, Chapter 2

1. I have used the term "shadowing" as it is used under the British parliamentary system of government, wherein the cabinet of the ruling political party is "shadowed" by the official opposition party. The opposition party functions as a government in waiting and appoints official critics (shadows) to the cabinet posts held by members of the governing party.

3 Invoking Our Highest Possibilities

THE HUMAN: A TRANSITIONAL BEING

As never before, new concepts are struggling to capture and interpret the impulse within humanity to give new expression to the meaning of human existence. To this end, we have seen contributions from various disciplines in the humanities and sciences. While this is a positive development — in that insights of one discipline concerning the fuller context of human reality usually find confirmation in other disciplines — there is a danger that we may see the transformational quest only in terms of the discipline through which we have become personally acquainted with it. The psychologist may see it only in terms of developing human potential, the sociologist in terms of new social alliances and structures, the ecologist in terms of a greater regard for Nature, and so on.

In order to navigate the variety of concepts and terms of reference surrounding the transformational quest, we need to see transformation in the broadest context possible. To see it only in one context may result in limiting our transformational potential. Since thoughts and concepts can either limit us or help us to focus our energy, we need to shape a perspective on transformation that will enable us to clearly assess how to translate the impulse into objectives of personal striving. Our goal must be to give the transformational impulse a place all its own within our aspirations and emotions.

From my perspective, the largest context for understanding transformation purports that the human species has not yet matured into what it must be. As Sri Aurobindo stated so well:

> Man is a transitional being; he is not final. For in man and high beyond
> him ascend the radiant degrees that climb to a divine supermanhood.
> There lies our destiny and the liberating key to our aspiring but
> troubled and limited mundane existence. . . .
>
> The step from man to superman is the next approaching achievement
> in the earth's evolution. It is inevitable because it is at once the
> intention of the inner Spirit and the logic of Nature's process. If earth
> calls and the Supreme answers, the hour can be even now for that
> immense and glorious transformation.[1]

In The Gospel According to Thomas, there is a curious little
parable that goes right to the core of how imperative it is for
humanity to cooperate with the transformational impulse. It
states: Blessed is the lion which the man eats and the lion will
become man; and cursed is the man whom the lion eats and the
lion will become man [Log. 7].[2]

This parable is as broad a context as we can find for the
transformational process. In the parable, the lion is a symbol for
Nature at the zenith of its physical perfection and its eagerness for
spiritual realization. Our role is to be trustee in charge of leading
Nature to spiritual realization. The imagery of the man eating the
lion represents the situation where mankind raises up all of
Nature. On the other hand, the imagery of the lion eating the man
represents a situation where humanity fails in the trust that Nature
has bestowed on it to lead the way toward realization.

In the parable, the lion is the winner in either case; it becomes
man whether it is eaten by man or eats man. This means that the
need of Nature to experience perfection will be fulfilled; it will not
be thwarted. Nature will accomplish its goal with or without
humanity.

However, even when we rise to the challenge that lies before us
to take a forward and upward step in consciousness, the problem
of how to proceed properly still remains. We need to clarify what
goals we must formulate and strive after. This will ensure that the
actions we take on behalf of the transformational impulse will be
appropriate.

INVOKING OUR HIGHEST POSSIBILITIES

In order to give our full support to the transformational impulse, we need first to define and delineate the impulse. This exercise has three aspects:

- First, we must get a feeling sense of the Universal Need behind the transformational impulse.

- Second, we must see that in the spiritual quest, each individual is a path.

- Third, we must develop a quality control procedure to help us determine Truth for ourselves. (Discussed in Chapter 4.)

Together, these three undertakings will help us invoke our highest possibilities by ensuring that the transformational impulse is given an identity all its own in our mental and emotional life, that it will have a representation there that gives it as much legitimacy, or even more, than other impulses that compete for release through our feelings and actions. Once we embark on these undertakings, we learn to discriminate between actions that are beneficial to the transformational impulse and promote its longevity, and those that stifle it.

The Universal Need behind the Transformational Impulse

It is important that we begin our facilitation of the transformational impulse at a conscious level by getting a sense of the Universal Need behind it. This will help us to perceive the spiritual quest as a call to universalize our being and not as something that makes us special. This distinction is crucial, because there are other psychic impulses which can mimic the transformational impulse and siphon off whatever nourishment is directed toward it. One of these is the *narcissistic complex*, which runs counter to the quest for meaning in life but can nevertheless masquerade within the psyche as the transformational impulse. The narcissistic complex manifests as the impulse towards sensations and is fueled by a perpetual state of boredom.

If we are under sway of the *dis*-ease of narcissim, we might feel that we are on the trail of some legitimate quest as we move from teacher to teacher, from tradition to tradition, and from path to path. The narcissistic complex makes it difficult for us to make commitments and take on responsibilities. Those of us who fall victim to it rationalize this mode of being by thinking that we are on the trail of something so important that we are exempt from ordinary responsibilities and commitments. We might honestly believe that the end justifies the means and that when the goal is reached, everything will be justified.

As we recognize the Universal Need that manifests itself as the transformational impulse, we learn to see how the impulse toward the transformation of consciousness has its origin in a Universal Design, within which any particular individual is only one stage of a long process. This process has a beginning far outside of our human conceptualizations, and it will resolve itself far beyond anything we can fully comprehend or even imagine. To get a feel for this Universal Need, it might help if we look at two examples. Our first example can be read from the "book" of Nature, and the second from a parable in the Old Testament book of Isaiah.

From the Book of Nature

For this example, we go to Point Pelee, a six-square-mile spit of land that juts out into Lake Erie and forms Canada's southernmost point. This spit of land creates a funnel for many migratory bird species as they fly to and from their wintering habitats. This stopover for birds gives bird-lovers a unique opportunity to observe more species than they could in an equivalent geographical area. It is said that up to one hundred bird species are sometimes observed here in a single day, and about three hundred species in a season. Birdwatchers, therefore, know that they are privileged to view the birds that use this particular spit of land, and for this reason they make the most of the season while it lasts.

We can find a similarity here between the transformational impulse manifested in humankind and the migratory impulse of birds manifested at Point Pelee. Just as a spit of land can become a stopover point for bird species, the individual human being can be regarded as a stopover of sorts, a certain crossover point for

Divine Energies. For us to neglect to probe further into the transformational impulse that is expressed through us would be equivalent to the bird-lovers who flock to Point Pelee taking the bird display as something staged specifically for their amusement. We would treat this as an unpardonable act of presumptuousness, should it happen, and regard such individuals as quite unbalanced. The offense is just as great if we fail to recognize the transformational impulse's impersonal element and regard it as our individual, personal project, to be expressed in whatever fashion we fancy.

Fortunately, the people who appreciate Point Pelee are intelligent enough to recognize that what is observed there is the expression of a "need" of Nature that they are privileged to observe. Although they do not control the flight paths of the birds, they realize that they could nevertheless help out by preventing impediments to this particular design of Nature. Point Pelee has been made a national park and a bird sanctuary, ensuring noninterference from bird enthusiasts and nonenthusiasts alike.

The Parable from Isaiah

The Old Testament prophet Isaiah gives us, in a very succinct parable, an insight into the Universal Design behind what we feel as the impulse towards meaning. Isaiah is speaking on behalf of the Divine Consciousness, whose Emanations stream forth into the phenomenal Universe and are expressed in humanity as just another stage of their expression. This prophet tells us:

> For as rain cometh down, and the snow from heaven, and returneth not thither, but watereth the earth, and maketh it bring forth and bud, that it may give seed to the sower and bread to the eater: So shall my word be that goeth forth out of my mouth: it shall not return unto me void, but it shall accomplish that which I please, and it shall prosper in the thing whereto I sent it (Is. 55:10–11).

Since the Divine Consciousness is not localized to a physical existence and thus does not have a literal mouth, the word that goes forth must be understood as Divine Energies, or the Divine Essence Itself. Although transformation is sometimes discussed in terms of evolution, in the sense that we unfold in potential, this does not fully consider the active role higher levels of reality undertake in this unfolding. To capture all the possibilities before us, we must think in terms of *symbiosis*. This idea defines a mutually supporting and sustaining relationship between different levels of life expression.

The Individual as a Path

From the perspective of symbiosis, the human being presents to another level of reality, which exists in another dimension, the opportunity to refine its expressions. Since we live in time–space, we can function as filters for a higher level of reality, allowing it to purge itself of characteristics incompatible with the unity of Life as a principle. In the process, it is able to refine itself further, and we grow in consciousness as a result.

Another aspect of this symbiotic relationship unfolds as we develop mastery of earthly life and become responsible in the way we handle freedom: the higher level of reality merges consciousness with us. This benefits the higher reality by allowing it to reap the benefits of experiences gained from the mastery of earthly life without having to go through all that we endured at the individual human level to gain that experience. In return, it bestows wholeness and authenticity of being on the individual through whom it has been able to fulfull itself. The life of the individual thus becomes validated and sanctified. This can be called Self-realization. It is in this sense that each individual is a path, because in reality the path to a transformed consciousness now becomes a case of minding the milieu created by the interaction of two different levels of reality.

This idea of a path is different to the way the path has been interpreted in esoteric traditions. In these traditions, it refers to a particular discipline that an individual may adhere to in order to bring about spiritual growth. Usually, a particular path implies a certain philosophical orientation and set of beliefs about the purpose of human life and guidelines concerning what we should target as goals and how to pursue them. In the classical sense, being "on the path" was the privilege of the very few. The vast majority of people lacked either the resources or the resolve to incorporate the quest for a higher consciousness into their everyday existence. This has changed, as large numbers of people, whose spiritual needs were satisfied by institutionalized religions in former times, are now finding such forms inadequate to meet the questions and challenges Life is placing before them.

Today, people from every walk of life are having experiences that in the past were reserved for mystics and occultists, and as a consequence are finding themselves catapulted into the search for answers to mysteries of which they had no notion previously. Because of this "democratization" of the transformational process in our day, the classical idea of a path as an externally imposed discipline no longer has exclusive validity, except in the broadest sense. If there are defined and trodden paths, they are to be found everywhere, in almost every vocation, in every economic class, in every place where people are found, on every mountain top, and in every plain or valley. This is because the expansion of consciousness does not restrict itself to man-made systems or conventions. In every respect, it is an autonomous process, with its own rhythm and laws.

A GLIMPSE OF OUR COMPLETENESS

My personal views on the transformational process began to coalesce following an experience I will now share. As a result of this experience, I now regard spiritual work not so much in terms of achieving a specific result, such as going somewhere or inheriting something, but in terms of the engagement of a process. It is my belief that if it were a single result that is required of our human experience, it could be accomplished in an instant, making all our present struggles and anguish unnecessary.

As for the experience itself, I can only relate it as I am able to recall it, not as I experienced it, as this is impossible. What I am sharing of this experience is paraphrased from what I was able to capture of it in my journal.

One morning, in 1976, I awoke in a swoon of ecstasy. I cannot now recall the circumstances surrounding my going to sleep the night before, but I do recall that this was a period of my life characterized by a very deep and intensive reflection on the course of my life. I was feeling a very profound sense of gratitude for the opportunities and blessings that were part of my life experience up to that time. This was accompanied by a very deep concern about the course of world events and about the meaning of human life.

The ecstasy I was experiencing on that morning permeated every pore of my body. It was also an ecstasy of mind and spirit, thoroughly integrated. I felt rested, peaceful, and above all, a lingering sensation of confidence. Although I was not able to fully comprehend the experience I had during the night, a thought became deeply etched in my consciousness. This thought, which fully summed up the experience, was something like this: IT IS ALL RIGHT.

As I lay in bed to allow my waking consciousness to take stock of this new sensation, the events of the night before began piecing themselves together. It seemed to me that some aspect of my being ascended to realms of existence very remote from everyday reality. During this sojourn, I was in the presence of Higher Beings who communicated telepathically with me and revealed insights that were somehow withheld from my analytical mind — in the sense that they could not be translated into specific thoughts and ideas. The only thought I was able to take with me from this experience was this sense of ALL RIGHT-ness. That thought alone summed up a new orientation to life acquired from the experience. I knew quite convincingly that there was order, logic, and meaning to all the haphazardness and incongruity that characterize life on the physical plane. I knew that God was in command, that He had a foolproof plan, that everything would work out for the Good, irrespective of the physical outcome.

While I continued to collect myself, steeped in ecstasy in the meantime, I felt that I had been made privy to a Great Secret, a Masterplan. I also recalled the sensation of that state somehow relating to luminous silver. It was as if the sensation of my own corporeal self was transformed into a molten, shining, glistening medium. There was no distinction between form, color, and sensation. There was also no question in my mind that I was experiencing an aspect of myself, albeit at a very impersonal level.

Because this experience was sudden and without precedent, I was unable to gain a perspective on it for some years. But even then, I was able to know what this experience *was not* more than what *it was*. During the course of the next six or seven years, a variety of other experiences of the lucid dream and astral travel categories allowed me to eliminate these as possible explanations. In none of these later experiences was my consciousness as refined as it was that morning. I felt that I genuinely had an insight into the very core of Life then, and although I had nothing objective to compare the experience to, I felt as though I had "ascended to Heaven." From then on I felt a great deal of affinity with the apostle Paul's writing about a man who was caught up into the third Heaven and who heard things not lawful for a man to repeat (II Cor. 12: 2–4). This is not to say that I am claiming an identical experience to that which Paul wrote about. But as Paul described, I was caught up into a state of consciousness where all knowledge was available to me and where some experience of identity remained; also, it was not "lawful" for me to repeat the communication I received — in the sense that the faculty was not there to capture and express in conceptual or verbal terms what was communicated.

Several months after this experience, I read *Life After Life* by Dr. Raymond Moody, Jr.,[3] and was able to see a parallel in some of the accounts there with my own. The main difference is that I did not have a near-death experience. Nor did I encounter a cultural representation of the Divine.

This experience has always served to bring me back to a feeling of hope for the world and for humanity whenever I lapse into feelings of despondency at the seeming predominance of negative forces such as greed, lust, cruelty, and general lack of concern one for another among us. Indeed, the world is bathed in incongruity and often appears to be only a poor reflection of the principles from which it derives its existence. However, the experience showed me that despite this surface darkness, the solutions to our world's problems already exist! It made me feel like a student who is allowed to have a peek at the solution to a mathematics puzzle. With the assurance that a solution to the problem exists, the student can go back and fill in the missing steps between the problem and its solution.

I feel that this is the point where we are in the state of the world. It is our role as individuals to give substance and form to this future that already exists. The meaning we give to individual transformation must come from this larger context of becoming channels and bridges that unite problems with their solutions. In this effort, an intermingling of forces is created — the result of the down-reaching of our Collective Future and the up-reaching of our consciousness at the individual level as we strive to improve ourselves. This becomes a Divine Milieu, where our efforts at the transformation of consciousness become a matter of being attentive to this milieu that we are hosting within. The implications of viewing transformation in this manner are many, and the most important ones are:

- Each one of us has an opportunity and a responsibility to make contact with one aspect of our Collective Future and to anchor it in the present.

- Transformation is a creative process, which allows each of us to bring something new into manifestation.

- As each one of us anchors one aspect of our Collective Future, we are jointly involved in our Collective Transformation.

Whatever personal meaning we give to transformation must come from the larger context of being bridges and channels to our Future, which already exists.

Notes, Chapter 3

1. Sri Aurobindo, "The Hour of God," in *The Essential Aurobindo*, ed. Robert McDermott (New York: Schocken Books, 1973), 55, 57.
2. A. Guillaumont et al., trans., *The Gospel According to Thomas* (New York: Harper & Row, 1959), 5.
3. Raymond A. Moody, Jr., M.D., *Life After Life* (New York: Bantam Books, 1976).

4 Getting Acquainted With Your Ideal Self

DEVELOPING A PERSONAL PHILOSOPHY OF LIFE

The next task at this phase of the work is for us to develop a quality control procedure by which we can discern truth for ourselves. This exercise is perhaps one of the most critical of the many that will be undertaken to ensure the longevity of the transformational impulse. Actually, by determining the elements that are to be part of our belief structure, we are consciously acquainting ourselves with our evolutionary future. It is the final act of distinguishing the transformational impulse from elements that are antagonistic to it.

The development of a personal philosophy of life is a way for us to focus our inner vision. We are really creating our own ideal being — defining what we would actually be if all the factors that stand in the way of our potential are removed. A personal philosophy requires that we commit ourselves to a particular way of viewing the world and take personal responsibility for our beliefs.

A personal philosophy must fulfill several requirements. It must bring us to some mental understanding of why we were born, help us to understand the present in terms of our past (i.e., relate cause and effect), and help us identify those principles of living that when applied, will enable us to meet life with confidence. All in all, a personal philosophy gives us a frame of reference for interacting with the world.

The exercise of developing a personal philosophy is similar to the skill of the archer as she perfectly lines up the arrow in her bow with the target. Even before the arrow is released, a perfect alignment of arrow and target means that they are in a type of contact — but for the passing of time. If our philosophy is a perfect fit and true reflection of what we can actually commit ourselves to in life, all it will take for us to become one with the ideal reflected by the philosophy is a commitment to express this philosophy in the earthly domain of time and action.

In deciding upon a philosophy of life, we may want to incorporate insights from various spiritual teachings and traditions. For this, a set of criteria is needed to allow us to choose in a consistent manner. There is nothing more self-defeating than holding various beliefs that may be contradictory to each other. It doesn't matter a great deal if we are only interested in philosophy as mental gymnastics; but in the context of our definition, we are seeking a belief system as a way of launching the complete being into life. And by this we mean finding a way to engage the various parts of our being in life in a meaningful way.

For me, the following eight criteria have proven useful in evaluating whether certain ideas and spiritual teachings should become part of my own beliefs. These are:

Relevance
Pertinence
Intentionality
Continuity
Verifiability
Consanguinity
Congruence
Objectivity

Relevance

The criterion of relevance asks us to enquire into the frame of reference or the context within which a system of ideas developed, and to ask whether that system can be taken out of its context and brought into our present situation without modification. A concept or a tradition that is not relevant to our present needs may end up creating more problems for us than it solves, in the same way that we might make ourselves sick if we take a medicine intended for an illness that we do not have.

Many of the religious teachings we find around us today were created thousands of years ago. In their natural, cultural contexts, they might have offered individuals an antidote to destructive attitudes and situations prevalent in their day. While such teachings may have been well-suited for a given level of human evolutionary development, they may be a millstone indeed for those of us who take them out of their contexts and adopt them without modification.

A good example of how knowledge of the context of a teaching can help is found in the doctrine of *karma* and *reincarnation*. Westerners who use this teaching to explain every conceivable hardship in life forget that the circumstances wherein this teaching took shape could have hardly resulted in any other view but the karma and reincarnation one. When we are surrounded by hardships and suffering at every turn, the easiest way to reconcile our experiences with the idea of a just and merciful God is to believe that all hardships are due to our past misdeeds. It is also a way of encouraging us to sow seeds of good deeds in the present for a better life in the future.

For us to have an understanding of Divine justice, it is unnecessary to subscribe to a literal understanding of karma and reincarnation. The paradox of Divine justice and the persistence of hardships and inequities among us can also be explained from a perspective based in the present life: *It is possible to see all the events in our life as operating to impress upon us the existence of ultimately only One Life.* We therefore attract all the circumstances of life that go together to orient us to the reality of this One Life.

If what I am saying is hard to accept, let us just consider for a moment how untenable are traditional ways of viewing karma and reincarnation. Let's say that an individual is born in a situation of wealth. Would we say that such an individual is enjoying good karma? If so, why do all the great teachers tell us that riches are a snare, or, as Jesus said, "It is easier for a camel to go through the eye of a needle than for a rich man to enter the Kingdom of God"? (Matt. 19:24)

When assessing a teaching, I suggest to everyone to try to understand the circumstances that gave birth to it and to see if those circumstances are still prevalent and whether the teaching may require a reformulation. How many of us continue to take a remedy for an illness that has long since ceased to exist?

Pertinence

With pertinence, we are concerned with how well a teaching fits our personal circumstances. This is similar to the criterion of relevance, except that with relevance we are concerned with the appropriateness of a teaching for a particular time and place. Here we are concerned with the appropriateness, for us, of a teaching that other people may find valuable. This criterion challenges us to see the transformational path as a very personal journey, where we must deal with the stuff of our own individual makeup. Spiritual understanding is progressive, and each of us must plug into the level that is right for our phase of development.

This criterion is particularly helpful when we are at the initial stage of acquiring a new lifestyle or a new "compass" to live by. We apply this criterion to assess the appropriateness, for us, of an external system by observing the people who are applying it. This does not mean that we judge them, only that we look closely to see the sort of need in them with which the teaching is resonating. I have personally applied this criterion over the years and have received no end of insight from doing so.

Intentionality

With the criterion of intentionality, we seek to know whether it is meaningful to set specific objectives of striving for ourselves when these objectives may be outside of our capacities to achieve them. In applying this criterion, we are assessing whether or not a goal of spiritual striving, decided at the level of the ego, is feasible. To illustrate the importance of this test, let us look at the concept of God-realization. One hears this concept mentioned quite often by Westerners who might have some acquaintance with yoga and Eastern philosophy.

Before we adopt this concept as part of our vocabulary, we

must ask what aspect of oneself realizes God. Under scrutiny, we see that God-realization cannot be a valid goal of spiritual striving, because God is not a reality that can be possessed. This is not to say that an individual cannot become a willing instrument of Divine Will. In this case, however, it is God that would be experiencing a realization through the individual. A more meaningful goal would be for the individual to seek to make her being a medium within which God can manifest.

The more we apply this criterion to the expectations we place on spiritual life, the more we are able to wean ourselves from a linear orientation to transformation. The linear approach treats the attainment of certain states of being that are not within human grasp as intentional pursuits. However, the only valid approach to incorporating higher realities is one that is successional. This means that we need to orient ourselves to transformation by ridding ourselves of all attitudes and expectations that are outmoded and outworn, or that we perceive at an intuitive level to be incompatible with our deepest insights and aspirations. With this orientation, the new consciousness we seek to realize will birth itself in us in proportion to the room we create for it in our beings.

Continuity

The criterion of continuity asks us to assess whether it is valid or meaningful to project our current sense of who or what we are (i.e., our sense of "me") into the future. Continuity requires us to identify that aspect of ourselves which is intended to benefit from specific experiences. When we apply this criterion we seek to determine what or who survives a specific experience. This enquiry is important, for it can be used to help us determine the extent to which ideas relating to reward and punishment, success and failure, karma and reincarnation, and so on, are meaningful at a personal level.

By using this criterion, we can ensure that the rationale we give ourselves for undertaking the journey of transformation is strong enough to provide us with an initial and sustained justification to stay with the journey. There are many concepts and teachings that may motivate us to begin the journey but which may not be sufficient to keep our attention focused on it. For example, teachings based on fear and enticement, such as Christian teachings of hellfire on one hand, and heavenly rewards on the other, may not be deep enough to enable us to find real meaning in life. For a teaching to assist us in finding real meaning, it must help us gain a perspective on the past, make sense of the present, and have hope for the future. The effect of a well-rounded teaching will be to assist us to organize our energies for real spiritual work.

Verifiability

In building a personal philosophy of life, we need to find a way to assess our own "revelations" so that we do not fall victim to self-delusion. Usually, an inner revelation is the hardest kind of information to validate, since we do not have the privilege of observing its effects on the lives of others who claim it as their own. This is all the more reason for inner revelations to be subjected to the acid test.

There are three simple ways of using the verifiability criterion in assessing a new piece of insight. First, we can assess it against what we have already proven, by experience, to be valid. Second, we can compare it against universally applicable principles to see if it violates any of them. Third, we can test this piece of insight or revelation by trying to see with the mind's eye what would happen if it became widely adopted in the world. If the result is one of disharmony, hate, and a decrease in general goodwill, then we will know that this revelation is lacking in universal applicability.

Even when things are not as clear-cut as above, we can still discern valid from invalid information of an internal nature by examining the possibility that an inner revelation might be a compensation for a hidden psychological need. We might feel that we have been selected as the expositor of a new doctrine or a new religion. Although it may not be stipulated, this may manifest an implicit desire to receive accolades, status, success. In order to avoid such a pitfall, we must see that true revelation is rarely, if ever, respectable. It is usually a risky business, since it requires its expositor to go against traditional norms. In circumstances of genuine revelation, the prophet is initially a reluctant messenger, not a volunteer.

Consanguinity

By consanguinity,[1] we mean the existence of equivalence. As a criterion, it requires us to recognize in action and a variety of settings the principles we are striving to incorporate into ourselves. Consanguinity is an important criterion in building a personal philosophy of life because, without it, we could be surrounded with knowledge and insights without being able to recognize their value, much less derive any benefit from them. Usually, when we initially embark on the quest to find meaning, there is a tendency to seek out the exotic, ignoring easily accessible information and living examples pertaining to what we are seeking.

Our chances of benefiting from applying this criterion grow as our familiarity with more than one religious or philosophical system increases. Versatility in this area will enable us to spot objective principles more clearly as they occur across different traditions and cultures.

Of the eight criteria, this one is the most important, because in applying it we learn to embrace concepts and principles that might help us understand our individual situations, as opposed to helping us reject the unacceptable. Consequently, it helps us to strengthen our intuition.

Congruence

With this criterion, we are concerned with the convergence or lack of convergence between a teaching or doctrine and our personal experience. In some respects, this criterion overlaps the others. However, its main value lies in getting us to utilize our critical judgment.

A case in point is the practice of some spiritual groups to program the mind with affirmations, which are then used as a substitute for direct personal experience. As an illustration, let us take the teaching of certain spiritual groups about duality. One variant of this teaching holds that spiritual seekers who cannot, like Jesus Christ, say "I and my Father are one" are subject to duality in their consciousness and consequently not in right attunement with God. They base this position on the belief that just as Jesus was able to acknowledge his Divine heritage and claim sonship with the Father, so too should every individual. To me, this misses the point entirely. In the first place, it takes too much literally and misses the symbolic truth in Jesus professing his unity with the Father aspect of the Godhead. At a symbolic level, Jesus represented *an archetypal energy of consciousness*, which is available to every individual but which may not be manifest in the consciousness of everyone. The archetypal energy of consciousness that Jesus modeled can say "I and my Father are one," because that is a way of acknowledging that divinity can be personal and transpersonal at one and the same time.

The verbal acknowledgment of unity with God therefore cannot and should not be a matter of affirmation or doctrinal faith. This is something to be experienced and embodied. If we are concerned about expressing unity with the Father aspect of the Godhead, we first have to embody the quality of consciousness that Jesus represented — the rest will follow. We will automatically be one with the Father.

I find it interesting that those individuals who go around saying "I and my Father are one" forget the first step — seeking unity with the archetypal Christ energy. The Christ energy or the Son aspect of the Godhead is the temporal expression of the Father, and in that sense, claiming unity with the Son exposes one to the critical evaluation of one's fellow human beings. On the other hand, claiming unity with the Father carries no such risk.

The application of this criterion would allow us to see that it is illogical to insist on unity with God only as the Primordial Unmanifest (i.e., Father) without also expressing that unity as the Temporal Manifest (i.e., the Christ aspect).

Objectivity

Objectivity is the final test. It asks us to step back and see how a belief or teaching looks from the "outside." By outside, we mean from outside the group, or the clique, or the culture that upholds it. Does the group explicitly or implicitly assume that its members are the recipients of special privileges? Do they somehow suggest that the Divine is the respecter of persons, that He or She or It holds favorites? This goes for our designation of the Divine as being of the male gender also. Throughout, I have spoken of God as He, but that is because of convention. For me, God is beyond gender.

If, as we apply the objectivity criterion, we find that if we've defined God as having favorites among us, some modification is clearly required to the doctrine or teaching we are adhering to.

The "Philosopher's Stone"

The application of these criteria will allow us to ground ourselves mentally and emotionally, and as a result, develop intuition. In this sense, these criteria, working together, become our philosopher's stone. By measuring every belief we have against this stone, we will bring the transformational impulse down to the level of daily attitudes and actions. When the transformational impulse is grounded in this manner, we help to create the necessary medium for the transformation of consciousness to facilitate itself. From here on, it becomes much easier to see how we can best cooperate with the Universal Design behind the transformational impulse.

Notes, Chapter 4

1. The term is derived from the word consanguine, which means "of one blood."

5   Toward Open-Ended Growth: Moving Beyond Roles and Goals

The next major step we must take in order to properly focus the transformational impulse is to begin relating to the transformation of consciousness as a holistic psychology. A holistic psychology is a psychology that is not oriented toward analyzing and fixing problems. Rather, its purpose is to help us achieve an orientation to Reality that is open-ended. This kind of psychology is crucial, because we cannot afford to wait until we've fixed all our problems before we proceed with the transformational journey. The application of a holistic psychology enables us to conduct our ideas about transformation through our aspirations, attitudes, and actions so that they can be tested at a practical level. Indeed, we may find that even though this kind of psychology is not problem focused, it will nevertheless help us to transcend and outgrow the psychological issues that may engage our attention at various periods of our life.

A spiritual or holistic psychology will eventually endow us with a spiritual orientation to life. Spiritual orientation is organic and is derived from the sense of center we experience from having cleared the lens of the mind and purified the heart. In some respects, we can compare spiritual orientation to the navigational instinct of migratory birds. Migratory birds have a built-in mechanism that enables them to find their way to and from their wintering habitats through vast distances and various weather conditions. So too, when we have acquired a spiritual orientation to life, we find ourselves being drawn toward the Good irrespective of the circumstances we may have to endure. It is only after this stage is reached that the transformational impulse becomes focused in our lives. Once we have become spiritually oriented in an organic way (i.e., with mind, emotions and will engaged in the transformational quest), we are motivated ongoingly toward a fuller and fuller integration of our human and spiritual endowments.

There are two main pillars to a holistic or spiritual psychology.

The first pillar is a sense of purpose in life — *a sense of what is possible for us as individual human beings.* Achieving a sense of personal purpose in life is also aided by having a personal philosophy of life. Because, as mentioned before, a philosophy is really a lifetime plan of action, and having a sense of personal purpose is just the engagement of that plan at an emotional level.

The second pillar of a holistic psychology is psychic integration. This is pursued by *incorporating attitudes within ourselves* that will create an emotional climate favorable to the longevity of the transformational impulse.

EXPERIENCING AND EXPRESSING PURPOSE IN LIFE

There are two basic perspectives from which we can approach the quest for a sense of purpose to our personal lives. We can seek *purpose in use* (or function), or *purpose in process.*

With purpose in use, we try to achieve our life's purpose in the pursuit of a goal, or in having a certain social position or societal role. With this orientation, we end up with all sorts of roles and goals that shape our idea of who we are. The consequence is that the distinction between outer aspects of our lives and our basic identities become blurred. The drawback of a role-oriented approach to finding life's purpose is the inevitable let-down that it leads to. When the role or the function to which we have bonded our identity is no longer needed, we feel useless. We see examples of this around us — the housewife who suddenly finds herself rudderless when her children have grown up and left home, the business person faced with bankruptcy, the professional faced with retirement or unemployment.

A sense of life's purpose, expressed in terms of use or function, is never permanent. It only postpones the inevitable — the day of reckoning, when we have to come to an intimate understanding of how we fit into the scheme of the entire Universe, not just a particular society or a given time and place. This day of reckoning usually occurs when some major letdown forces us to find meaning to our life greater than the interactions we have with our given society. At this point we might be ready to relate to our life's purpose in terms of process.

Relating to our life's purpose in terms of process focuses the transformational impulse by orienting us in the direction of open-ended growth rather than toward fixed goals. Goals may still play a significant part in our life expression, but they function only as milestones — targets to be exceeded. The most obvious benefit of an open-ended growth orientation is that we do not allow ourselves to feel devastated when our roles change or when we fail to achieve a goal. By being open to the possibilities of failure in our personal endeavors, we maximize our opportunities for growth.[1] For we discover that it may actually be in the interest of the transformational impulse if some goals are not achieved. When we begin to lend our conscious cooperation to the transformational process, we may, out of excitement, set goals of striving that may not be adequately thought out. Such goals, although they may represent a forward developmental step from where we are at a given moment in time, may not be altogether appropriate from a higher level of awareness. In effect, when we formulate goals and targets of striving, we do so in semi-light, and we must retain the flexibility to reassess these goals as the light of awareness becomes brighter and as our spiritual vision becomes clearer.

When we experience a sense of our life's purpose that is not dependent on roles and goals, we are able to become fully engaged in life (i.e., daily activities) and, as a result, are able to experience Life (i.e., as a principle) independently of our limiting definitions of ourselves. We also become aware that we touch Life at a unique point, in line with our capacities, gifts, and aspirations. From here on, by consecrating all of our experiences to the whole of Life,[2] we begin to receive revelations of spiritual principles in our inner being. With an orientation such as this, we experience our life's purpose as a progressive unfolding of being and a progressive acquaintance with Truth. Truth, in this sense, is to be understood as an inner attunement to Reality, to wholeness, rather than in terms of a particular doctrine or specific set of ideas. It is when such a relationship is engaged that we relate to Life from a truly spiritual perspective.

The eventual outcome of a process-oriented sense of purpose is an appreciation of the unique part each one of us can play in expressing and anchoring a facet of our Collective Future. We also provide the means through which our Collective Future is brought into expression when we take personal responsibility for our vision of a better way of living. Through such personal responsibility, we function as interdimensional "birth canals" for our Collective Future. A process-orientated approach to purpose is therefore both personal and transpersonal.

A personal incident from my life provides a clear example of how purpose in process expresses itself. For several years I carried a notepad with me to jot down my ideas and intuitions on the spiritual quest. I did this everywhere — in restaurants, on buses and trains, at work, and at home. I would later type out these notes, developing the ideas a bit more as I did so. Sometimes I would have enough to fill one or two typewritten pages at a time. At time of writing, I did not have a specific goal in mind, Actually, I had no "use" for these notes in the sense that I did not know what I would do with them. I wrote in this fashion for several years. Eventually, I began writing full-time and found that I was able to use these earlier pieces in my current projects with very few changes. Natural gaps would occur in my writing where my earlier pieces fitted quite organically and smoothly. This present book is also the beneficiary of some of these earlier writing efforts.

Although these pieces of writing were complete in their own way, when incorporated in a larger work, such as a book, they obtained a greater congruence and integrity; outside of the overall context of a book, they might have remained just unrelated and individual pieces. When we dedicate ourselves unreservedly to the transformational impulse, becoming fully committed to serving the principle of Life without worrying about results, we eventually become uplifted to function as part of a larger Reality. A sense of purpose that is process-oriented is therefore a sense of being creatively engaged in life. Rather than basing our activities on their status value, we base them on our need to give expression to our soul nature. Thus engaged, our commitment to principles replaces our need for specific outcomes as our prime motivation.

THE QUEST FOR PSYCHIC INTEGRATION

Simply put, psychic integration is a sense of being or an experience of center that takes our spiritual aspects into account. Integration is an essential step in the transformation of consciousness, for without some experience of center, there is no point of reference in the psyche around which a new life orientation can be anchored.

Self-Acceptance

Integration begins with self-acceptance, which is itself a form of integration. This is one of the key paradoxes of transformation, so aptly expressed by the medieval alchemists in the statement that *one needs gold to make gold*. The basis of self-acceptance is our willingness to accept ourselves as we are.[3] It is an inward movement of making peace with oneself, which is only possible when we are able to relate to our own life and its contents from a place of neutrality. Self-acceptance involves our capacity to see ourselves in a balanced perspective — to be able to see our faults alongside our virtues and our weaknesses alongside our strengths. Once we've accepted ourselves, we no longer punish ourselves for subscribing to standards we currently feel incapable of maintaining. At the same time we do not downgrade our ideals and aspirations just because we currently experience difficulty giving expression to them. Self-acceptance allows us to get a view of the organic flow of our life as opposed to the content of our life at any given period.

Self-acceptance enables us to be patient with ourselves, thereby creating an emotional climate hospitable to integrating the various scattered parts of the self. This is essential for transformation, because transformation takes place from the inside outwards. In the absence of some meaningful level of integration, and therefore a sense of center, we will continue to be torn by competing impulses, resulting in the fragmentation of our psychic energy.

It is important that we approach self-acceptance as an act of humility. Affirmations that force self-acceptance as a pretended stance gloss over our weaknesses just like wallpapering over cracks in a wall. There is a danger that such a stance can do violence to the organic movement of intrapsychic reconciliation within ourselves by making acceptance, whose true character is humility, into something resembling arrogance.

The Immersion Process

The path to integration means becoming enveloped in something greater than ourselves. The quest for integration is therefore an adventure of faith, as it allows one to lose oneself continually, to find the self again in a larger context. In essence, this is an immersion process, and to navigate our way through it we must keep our attention focused on our deepest aspirations and those aspects of our life that are functioning in cooperation with these aspirations. This exercise is also an aspect of self-acceptance, and the more we learn to factor the highest parts of our nature into waking consciousness, the more we are able to trust, and to release the fretting anxieties we experience as a result of being engaged in the immersion process.

To stay in the immersion process that leads to integration, we need to engage all of our being, not just part of it, in the process of transformation. It is this full engagement that makes the process an immersion and a passage. This approach to transformation is quite distinct from approaches solely concerned with techniques. Techniques do not engage the whole being in the transformational process, since some parts need to stay behind to wield the technique and assess the progress. In this sense, purely technical approaches to transformation eventually become strategies to get what we want from life from an egotistical perspective. The eventual result of an ego-directed, technical approach to transformation is further fragmentation of the being.

On the surface, approaches that emphasize techniques appear less threatening than the approach of immersion. Sole reliance on techniques leads us to expect to achieve something tangible after the technique has been mastered. On the other hand, in the immersion approach, we see only sacrifices and effort, with no reward in sight. This is not altogether false, for immersion can indeed bring pain. This is the pain of discipline, of humiliation, that we may experience as our body, mind, and ego resist losing their autonomy. Until the new disciplines become natural to the whole being, individual components of our being will revolt.

The transformational process may also be painful as a result of past programming. In their ordinary state of functioning, the physical, emotional, and mental parts of our being are organized to seek happiness as the arch-purpose to life. However, when immersion into the transformational process occurs, happiness may appear rather elusive, and we may experience negative tension[4] in our being. Until the idea of personal happiness as the main goal of life is corrected, the strain resulting from immersion into the transformational process will frustrate this goal, and we may experience difficulty getting the lower aspects of our being to cooperate. In reality, happiness is only possible when a part of our being is living in the past, where it compares the present with some past state. Making happiness the goal of life assumes that the quality of our being does not change, but remains static, while only conditions change. Psychologically speaking, the goal of happiness involves placing too much currency in our memories. In the pursuit of meaning in life — which is what the transformational process is really about — we must acclimate to change. Unlike the pursuit of happiness, which is always defined in the context of some prespecified condition, the quest for meaning always takes us into the unknown.

Integration Vectors

As a practical discipline, integration must be pursued along two vectors. These two vectors of integration relate to time and space but can also be considered as vertical and horizontal.

The temporal vector of integration is engaged when we internalize our conscience and develop equanimity. The engagement of the temporal vector gives us inner composure such that we do not constantly regret some past action or lack of one, or agonize over some future action to be taken. In terms of a tangible focus, we further the process of integration along this vector when we work at unbinding and recycling those portions of our psychic energy that have been appropriated by feelings of guilt and anxiety.

The objective of pursuing integration along its temporal vector is to enable us to live in the present. As we approach this state of being we find that more and more of our actions, taken or contemplated, emanate from our essence and therefore leave less and less cause for regret or fear of the future.

We pursue integration along its spatial vector by striving to achieve mental clarity and an openness to new possibilities. When we are clear and open in this manner, we do not expend our energy defending fixed positions, nor do we spread ourselves so thin that the force of our will cannot be brought to bear on a matter that is important to us. In other words, the spatial vector of integration gives us the ability to achieve *mastery over our attention*. We are able to take our attention from one matter and place it on another whenever we determine that a certain matter has more importance to more of our being than another.[5] By continually exercising this faculty, we learn to prioritize our activities in line with our values and, as a result, bring the true essence of our being into daily life.

FEEDING THE PROCESS TOWARD INTEGRATION

Dealing with Guilt

To deal with guilt effectively we need to look into the dynamics of its pathology. We must begin with the emotional state of affairs that started the chain of events that culminates in a feeling of guilt. Often, this is an absence of forethought. We act without giving due consideration to the consequences, so the result is regret. What we recognize as guilt is the emotional and organic effects of afterthought (i.e., dwelling on the past) expressing themselves in a certain set of symptoms. Where there is forethought, there is less occasion for afterthought, and consequently, less possibility of guilt. To deal with guilt effectively we must begin by dealing with afterthought.

Guilt arises after a deed because we realize that we possessed or had access to more information than we took into consideration when we performed that deed. We are reminded of this by our conscience. Sometimes we deal with afterthought by silencing our conscience, but this is like punishing the messenger for bringing the bad news. A more constructive approach is to balance the conscience with a commitment to change and exercise more responsibility. This will also effectively silence the voice of conscience, but in a positive sense. Conscience is effectively silenced only when we return to a psychological state of *innocence*, which is the only true antidote for guilt.

It is possible to return to innocence from guilt when we are able to retroactively change the motivation behind an act. This is not a game or some mental sleight of hand where we try to justify our mistakes after the fact, but an exercise where we explore the full potential of an action, for self-understanding. This leads to an increased commitment to our own growth. If an experience has contributed to our growth by giving us a fuller understanding of the transformational process and a greater commitment to it, then the doer who originally committed the deed no longer exists, and the present person is genuinely psychologically innocent. In other words, when we are able to acknowledge our mistakes and learn from them, we derive benefits from those very mistakes. Our mistakes become like pieces of stone that birds ingest with their food, to aid their digestion.

Each one of us can identify situations in our life where mistakes have opened up new horizons for understanding our human condition. In this regard, I am reminded of the following line from Sri Aurobindo's epic poem *Savitri*: "[God] made error a door by which Truth could enter in."[6]

Dealing with Anxiety

The medical causes of anxiety are numerous. However, its effects are the same irrespective of its many causes. Anxiety thwarts the maintenance of psychic and spiritual integration by making us live in the future to the detriment of our awareness of the present. The cure for anxiety is to develop a sense of trust in the transformational process. This gives us equanimity. Actually, if we take the time to review our life we would see situations where we have triumphed even though we did not think at the time that we would possibly survive. When we look at our own bodies we see an inherent wisdom at work: organs and systems work without our conscious interference; the body heals itself of diseases, most times unaided by medicines. In our anxious moments we will do well to remember this key line from God's answer to Job's protestations: Where were you when I laid the foundation of the earth? (Job 38:4).

To trust God, or the transformational process, does not mean that all the events of life will turn out according to our expectations: *Our expectations of Life are no guide as to what ought or ought not to happen to us.* Quite simply, we rarely know what is right for us. How many times have we experienced what appears to be a disappointment only to find later that it was a blessing in disguise? When trust is present we are assured that as long as our motivation is pure, the action and consequences it leads to will result in the growth of our consciousness. Instead of focusing on and being insistent about the results we want from a situation, we will best serve the transformational impulse if we continually examine our motives for our actions. We need to be always asking ourselves: Am I acting from spiritual principles or for ego fulfillment?

When we are able to curb fretting anxieties, more energy becomes available to bring more of our essence into the present. One of the things we should always bear in mind is that the transformation we are working at is both personal and collective. There are times when we may be called upon as individuals to be a living example to fellow seekers so that we can inspire them to nurture and facilitate the transformational impulse in themselves. The way we handle disappointments and vexing situations can usually trigger a similar response in others. I have personally found the following reminder quite helpful when I am faced with disappointments and apparent setbacks: *My personal life is not an end unto itself. I must strive to see and be open to the Greater Good of which this situation is only a building block.*

SPIRITUAL ORIENTATION

Earlier, we compared spiritual orientation to the navigational instinct of migratory birds. This analogy is not without merit, for at a practical level the engagement of the temporal and spatial vectors of integration will leave their impact in the psyche in the form of two distinct attitudes, which will help us change our orientation to life from a materialistic to a spiritual one.

Since the eventual outcome of pursuing integration along its temporal vector is the internalization of conscience and the development of equanimity, the attitude toward transformation fostered by this vector is that of relating to the transformative journey as one indivisible unit. This means that there is no separation of means and ends in our approach to transformation. Consequently, the pursuit of integration along its temporal vector enables us to *live in the present.*

Pursuit of the spatial vector of integration (which deals with gaining mastery over our attention and organizing our life according to our priorities) will precipitate the attitude wherein *we give an open option to the Divine Spirit, to God.* With this attitude, we do not place desire images in the way of the transformational impulse by holding preconceived ideas of how it should personally benefit us.[7]

Living in the Present

With the internalization of conscience and equanimity, which are the fruits of pursuing integration along its horizontal or temporal vector, we free ourselves from the influences of the past and future on our current actions and become capable of living in the present. Normally, our acts are either the end result of actions taken or promised earlier or predicated on future developments that we are willing to accept. The result is that we never really act consciously, but are always *re*-acting. But with temporal integration, our actions are governed by a clear understanding of a particular principle that we are putting into action, rather than by motivations based upon reward or fear. In the context of the transformational process, we undertake actions because of our commitment to the transformational process in its broadest scope.[8] Consequently, we act more from a sense of what is necessary to keep us at the frontier of our transformational possibilities than from what is required to produce a particular end result.

When we relate to the whole transformative journey as one indivisible unit, we will have acquired equanimity. At a feeling level, this attitude resembles the existential condition that someone who is awaiting the birth of a baby may experience. In a delivery room, members of the attending party have to come to terms with two competing realities that are vying for their attention and sympathy. They know that there is a baby to be born, but they also know that they have to apportion their attention and sympathy between the suffering mother and the baby desiring to be born. Should they be preoccupied with the baby itself and be concerned only with facilitating a quick birth? Or should they be primarily concerned with alleviating the pain of the mother and risk the suffocation of the baby? Neither of these either/or scenarios is acceptable: It is possible to have a live and healthy baby and a welcoming and appreciative mother. Similarly, on the transformational path, we have to learn how to apportion our sympathy between the various realities in our charge.

There is an old riddle that most appropriately poses the dilemma that the person playing host to the transformational impulse must face. In this riddle, a man is faced with the problem of transporting a wolf, a goat, and a cabbage across a river in a boat that can only take him and one other of his charges at a time. The problem is that he can never leave the goat and the cabbage unattended since the goat will eat the cabbage, nor could he ever leave the wolf and the goat unattended since the wolf will devour the goat. He must devise a strategy that ensures that all cross the river safely. The principle that figures most prominently in the solution to this dilemma is patience and the willingness of the man to "walk the second mile," which, in this case, consists of crossing the river an extra time.[9]

The existential condition equivalent to the situations posed by the birth analogy and the riddle is this. As we begin to acquire knowledge and experiences that accompany our cooperation with the transformational impulse, knowledge and experiences can further fragment the being by alienating that part of ourselves that cannot participate in them. It will be necessary for us to live with our lower nature for a while without truncating it.[10] Truncation might bring initial success, but we will encounter resistance later on as repressed aspects rebound in full force. Also, we have to be careful that as our aspirations dwell on our possibilities, we do not capitulate the throne of Selfhood in our life to an imposter. This occurs when we accept an incomplete or false realization as the final goal of transformation. We have to be careful that our acquaintance with only a minute aspect of the Self does not lead to an imbalance. Knowledge must be balanced with understanding, which comes from doing; aspiration must be grounded in humility and compassion; vision must be tempered with knowledge of the world as it is. All in all, we must be aware of the difference between what is possible for us as individuals and what is possible for a larger humanity at a given time in our collective awakening.

Moving from an Acquisitive to an Eliminative Consciousness

Giving *an open option to God* in our transformational quest is the practical outcome of an openness to new possibilities and our ability to shift our attention from matters of low priority to matters of high priority, in the transformational sense. Giving an open option to God means that we do not direct our efforts at transformation toward any specific goal or end point. Instead we regard the end of one stage of the journey as the beginning of another. By doing this, we move from an orientation in consciousness that is *acquisitive* to one that is *eliminative*. This new orientation in consciousness is necessary if we are to solve one of the foremost problems that plague us on the transformational path: How do we maintain our interest in transformational matters as a quest for wholeness, as opposed to just another ego pursuit with the promise of some gigantic payoff?

When we view transformation as a quest with a reward in the end, we may fail to involve all of our being in the process. A part of us is kept back to anticipate what it will be like when the task is completed. It really doesn't matter how subtle the nature of the reward — eternal salvation, development of human potential, psychic powers, enlightenment, God–realization, whatever. The underlying assumption to all expectations of reward is that at the end of a given period of effort we are left with something that, upon reflection, would make us feel that it was worthwhile to have expended the effort or undertaken certain sacrifices. If we fail to give an open option to the process, we become further fragmented, because we end up being too acquisitive in our orientation to transformation. The approach that will take us through the process safely is an eliminative one. With an acquisitive approach, we are concerned with adding to what we already have, whereas with the eliminative approach, we are focused on getting rid of what is not truly of our deeper Self.

When we have an acquisitive orientation to transformation, we expose ourselves to two hazards. The first hazard is in the form of the temptation to settle upon a false or incomplete realization as an indication of final spiritual attainment. In reality, we can never know in advance how the journey will be consummated; we can only know that in retrospect. For this reason, an egotistic attachment to achievements and rewards entices one to "jump the gun," as the saying goes. The second hazard is in the condition I will label *asymptosis*. This word is derived from the mathematical concept, the asymptote, which defines a relationship between a curve and a straight line in which the curve approaches the line at such an angle that it gets ever closer but is unable to touch it on this side of infinity.

Asymptosis in spiritual life occurs when our expectations get in the way so that we can never directly realize that for which we are striving. When, instead of expecting specific results, we given an open option to the Divine Spirit, to God, we are content to leave it up to God to complete us in whatever way He sees fit. Whether our transformational journey leads to obscurity or fame, abundance or subsistence, we must be willing to accept the transformation on its own terms, not on our own. *Unless this openness is present, we will find ourselves resisting the very same thing for which we are supposedly striving.* Such is the inevitable result of relating to transformation as something to be acquired or to be added to that which we have already achieved of a worldly nature. Even knowledge is included here, because it can be one of the chief offenders.

When we truly create room for the transformational impulse to grow, we find that the only true claim we can make regarding knowledge is that we know less and less. And ironically, this is the type of climate that is most beneficial to the longevity of the transformational impulse because, in a state of *unknowing*, we rediscover what it means *to wonder*. At a practical level, giving an open option to the process means that we are able to say to the Mystery that is God, "*Thy will be done!*"

Notes, Chapter 5

1. If we cannot admit to the possibility of failure, we will abstain from situations and pursuits where success is not guaranteed or where there is even the slightest possibility that we may not realize our objectives. Consequently we miss out on new experiences and numerous opportunities for growth.

2. Dedicating something to the whole life means not to personalize it but to relate to it from the perspective of principle. The "whole of life" includes expressions of life that exist outside the range of our personal preferences.

3. Accepting ourselves "as we are" involves accepting full responsibility for everything that we are. Self-acceptance includes the full range of experiences of the Self, with both the Higher and Lower Self. Full self-acceptance therefore means that we acknowledge and accept our survival needs, but not at the expense of our transcendental needs (finding meaning in life, relating to the Universe and God, etc.). Self-acceptance is therefore a balancing point between the opposing psychic tensions of being and becoming. Consequently, any attempt at self-acceptance without bringing the higher reaches of our nature into the picture amounts to living in a fool's paradise.

4. Negative tension results from resistance and produces anxiety, psychosomatic pain, insomnia, etc., whereas positive tension results from the creative process.

5. A simple example of how we can exercise mastery over our attention to the benefit of more of our being is the choice of deciding which of two activities to engage in. Let us take, for example, the decision between watching an entertaining program on television and reading a book on psychology or philosophy. The part of ourselves that wants to watch television might tell us that we should relax in front of the television, and it may rationalize that we are tired, have had a long day, etc. And indeed we may begin to feel fatigued as we listen to this voice. On the other hand, the part of us that wants to read knows that new insights with long-lasting benefits could be gained, much longer lasting than the instant gratification of watching television. So we decide to read the book. Lo and behold, as soon as we start reading, we find we are no longer tired, but energized as a result of the mental stimulations from the insights we are exposed to.

6. Sri Aurobindo, *Savitri — A Legend and a Symbol* (Pondicherry, India: Sri Aurobindo Ashram Trust, 1972), 625.

7. We may have a tendency to regard the transformational quest as an apprenticeship to become a teacher or guru. To be fully committed to the transformational process, we must regard it as a process of human maturation for which compensation is the process itself.

8. This means that we are motivated by the transformational process in its universal scope, which is the evolution of our species and the realization that we have no real choice but to cooperate with this process.

9. For those not familiar with this riddle, this is the solution: The man takes the goat across to the other side, leaving the wolf and the cabbage. He returns for the wolf, takes it across, but brings the goat back with him. He leaves the goat and takes the cabbage across. He then leaves the wolf and cabbage together and returns for the goat. He takes the goat across and all are reunited. He makes four trips in total, even though he has only three charges, but this is necessary to keep them all intact.

10. It is sometimes difficult to know when we are truncating parts of our being, since we do not do this consciously. It occurs through the process of denial — we believe we have outgrown an immature character trait. However, we may exhibit an intolerance and lack of compassion toward others in whom we recognize these same traits. A sure way of discovering what we are truncating in ourselves is to observe our judgmental attitudes toward others. Those aspects of character and behavior of which we are most critical in others suggest what we may be denying in ourselves. If we have truly outgrown our areas of immaturity, we will regard others with the same degree of compassion we show toward our past selves.

6   Meditation: Counteracting Fragmentation, Inertia, Self-Interest, and Ignorance

"A journey of a thousand miles begins with one step," says a well-known Chinese proverb. Nowhere is that statement more pertinent than in our urge to transform our consciousness. Despite grand schemes and noble ideals, transformation boils down to how we engage our attention and make use of the sixty-five thousand seconds that make up the average waking day.

It is not that we have to attempt the impossible task of keeping a running account of these waking moments, but rather we must take some initiative to predetermine their use. This can be done by instilling attitudes and behavior in our beings that are consistent with our transformational ideals. We know how difficult it is to break a habit that commits us to a negative pattern of behavior once it is acquired. What may not be so obvious is the ease with which good habits also gather momentum and ·perpetuate themselves. When it comes to predetermining the ways in which the moments of our lives are utilized, "What is sauce for the goose is also sauce for the gander" — the same habit-forming dynamic in consciousness that commits us to destructive behavior routines also allows us to cultivate constructive behaviors.

To keep the transformational process on track we must commit ourselves to daily practices. Such practices are very much like inputs of energy into a piece of machinery in order to sustain motion. To keep a bicycle going uphill, for instance, we have to pedal it, or to keep a motorcar running, gasoline must be fed to its engine. This is necessary in order to counteract a natural tendency of the machine to slow down and stop. With us humans, things are very much the same. We have to continuously counteract tendencies towards inertia, narrow self-interest, and ignorance. All of the other lapses with which we are plagued stem from these three basic ones. They are the direct result of our "marooned" existence in a three-dimensional world of time, space, and matter. We therefore need particular practices in order to maintain a frame of mind conducive to the longevity of the transformational impulse. One of the practices we have to cultivate in order to entrench values in the being that help facilitate the transformational impulse is that of meditation.

MEDITATION AS A WAY OF LIFE

The last quarter of a century has seen an influx into Western culture of many practices that go by the name of meditation. It is quite difficult for the nonpracticing enquirer to get an unambiguous answer as to what meditation is in its most basic expression. There seems to be a bias to describe meditation in terms of techniques rather than as a way of life. Depending upon who is consulted, we might be told about transcendental meditation, zen meditation, kundalini meditation, sufi meditation, yoga meditation, and many more varieties.

What we might want to know, as when I first enquired about the subject, is whether there is a generic meaning to the concept of meditation that may cut across all the cultural factors that surround it. When I enquired into meditation years ago, I was looking for the *philosophy* of meditation. I wanted to find what it is that meditation is supposed to do for me and to what common end all of the various methods of meditation are supposed to take me.

People who study meditation in a scientific sense seem to be concerned only with the *psychology* of meditation. That is, they limit their research to the measurement of changes in feeling states and perception, and to changes in certain vital body signs. The concerns that the philosophy of meditation addresses are much larger than these. The philosophy of meditation seeks to find out what it is in us that meditation seeks to put to right, and how different methods of meditation relate to various configurations of our inner needs.

The basic assumption behind all methods of meditation is that one is in a state of *fragmentation*. In this fragmented state, we are unable to bring all of our parts together to work in unison for the good of the whole being. These various parts exist as warring factions so that we may lose effectiveness in many areas of life. We are unable to organize our life in the material world so that it corresponds with our ideals and aspirations. We may, out of forgetfulness, timidity, distractions, and fear, find that we are unable to follow through with actions that are designed to help bring about a betterment of our life. We may also find that other actions may occur quite on their own, despite our best efforts not to let them manifest themselves. These latter actions may be recognized as habits, compulsions, attractions and repulsions, and possibly neuroses.

First Stage — Coming to Grips with Our Ideals and Aspirations

The practice of a generic meditation, i.e., meditation as a way of life, will help us to bring an end to fragmentation and restore effectiveness to our greater will.[1] In the initial stages of practice, we must try to come to grips at an emotional level with the implications of our ideals and aspirations. We must try to bring ourselves to experience, in as realistic a way as possible, a situation that is not yet material. It is essential that we first experience the kind of world that we aspire to as a possibility, at a mental level. Only when we've reached this stage can the rest of our being cooperate with our desire for integration and effectiveness.

Our effort to get an emotional reading on what it is we are aspiring for also becomes a test of our sincerity. Quite simply, if we do not have a sense, at an emotional level, of what our ideals imply in a practical sense, then the ideals will not really be part of our being, but could be merely a set of ideas pirated from others. We usually pick up ideas without going through the rigorous mental exercise of working out conclusions for ourselves. Should this be the case with our spiritual ideals, we find that when the occasion arises for our ideals to be challenged, we falter in our commitment.

A clear distinction must be made here between the task of

getting an emotional grip on our ideals and aspirations and what is commonly called visualization. This latter practice has validity in its own right for matters less critical than the restoration of spiritual integration. The emotional reading we are after is more in line with an accounting exercise to determine what our ideals and aspirations imply at a practical level. This exercise is similar to what Jesus suggested we do before we embark on the spiritual quest. We are advised to emulate the leader of an army that is readying for battle: Just as he must assess the strength of his army against that of the enemy, we also ought to get a sense of the degree of moral fortitude we will require to give birth to our spiritual ideals.

Second Stage — Commitment to Action

The second stage of generic meditation is reached when we commit ourselves to making personal adjustments in our life. Unless we do this, contemplation on our ideals and their practical implications becomes pointless. It is only when we ground our spirituality in practical changes in our everyday affairs that the channels between our possibilities and our present situation are cleared. Our willingness to make practical adjustments is an indication that we are ready to receive fresh insights from the Higher Self.[2]

If we practice any form of meditation with the sole objective of getting some form of mystical experience, we may bypass the greatest possible benefit of meditation while being preoccupied with incidentals. The benefit of meditation is in assisting us to unite our fragmented being and build a new foundation for an integrated life, a new life. We can only achieve this benefit when we see the objective of meditation as the unification of a fragmented being. In this regard, meditation helps us to *re-member* ourselves and acts as the gateway to spiritual consciousness. If we are not concerned with personal change, but instead seek experiences for their own sake, our situation becomes like that of a tourist who visits a foreign country as often as possible with no intention at all of ever settling there. He is forever a tourist.[3] To commit to the type of meditation recommended here is like familiarizing ourselves with the new country, with its ways, its laws, its customs, its ideals, etc., because we are planning to make our home there.

There is a danger for those of us who practice meditation only for the adventure of it and are not prepared to make changes to our lives. Our beings will become clogged with undigested ideals and beliefs. Such unprocessed energies will eventually lead to mental and emotional confusion, and possibly delusion. The real tragedy, though, is that we may go through life full of all sorts of ideas and beliefs that may each be quite dear to us, but when taken together may be antagonistic one to the other. Unfortunately, we may not see that our various beliefs are incompatible, since it is only when we make the effort, first to derive the emotional or feeling state that a particular belief or idea implies, and second, to attempt to conduct ourselves in a manner consistent with the belief, that we discover any other ideas and beliefs we have that are contradictory to it.

As we conduct our meditation in the manner suggested here, we make the important discovery that genuine meditation is not separate from the rest of our life. In saying this, I am aware that there are those people who may relate to various forms of meditation in terms of an immediate, usable benefit such as stress reduction, for instance. While there is nothing wrong with stress-reduction exercises as such, the question that we must ask ourselves is whether we are reducing the stress in our lives just so that we can go back into the world to continue doing the same things that are stress-provoking. Here I am reminded of a cartoon showing a woman on a psychiatrist's couch with the caption, "Doctor, I already know that I am burning my candle at both ends. I am here for more wax." Granted that the nature of our technological society is such that we are constantly exposed to stressful situations, we must nevertheless be on the alert for opportunities to take more of our essence into the marketplace. This might have a price in terms of lost prestige or a loss of competitive edge from the standpoint of the world. But this price is a small one if our meditation practice is to lead us to the goal of integration. Eventually, our meditation practice becomes so spontaneous that even ordinary living will become mediation. We will have achieved meditation with open eyes!

Third Stage — Becoming Master of Our Attention

To the extent that generic meditation helps us to bring our ideals down to the mental level and into our daily activies, *we become more of what we are, in essence, and less of what we are not.* This is what it means to have true will: It is that which enables us to become individuals in the true sense of the word. It helps us to bring our many scattered parts together so that they can work in unison. Without will, we remain fragmented and always experience destructive tension in our beings.

In its role of assisting us to remember our values and ideals, meditation functions like a gyroscope. Just as a gyroscope allows one to achieve and hold a relationship of balance with respect to a level surface, minding the moments of our life assists in orienting us in terms of the grand ideals we hold for ourselves. If our ideals cannot find an entrance into the moments of our life, then they might as well be discarded as superfluous. Only when we have a relationship with these moments are we able to instill in our being habits and actions consistent with such personal ideals.

SHARED PERFECTION

The three stages of this approach to meditation harmonize the functions of three independent levels of our being: spirit, mind, and body. As we harmonize spirit, mind, and body, we are bringing three separate wills into harmony. When these three wills are brought into alignment, the result is an averaging out of the being so that no particular aspect gets the upper hand. This averaging is a key milestone of the spiritual quest, since it is more essential to achieve harmony in the way different parts of us function than to selectively develop particular facets of ourselves.

In essence, the averaging process means that at the spiritual level, we may not be able to fully capture our aspirations into a philosophy of life; at the mental level, we may be unable to gain a full perspective on how to translate our philosophical ideals into a plan of action; at the physical level, we may have to live with resistances in the body in regard to its cooperation with the tasks the mind may outline for it. We have to acknowledge that we may have to live with imperfection; but by the same token, we will realize that *it is far better to actually engage in the construction of a molehill than to contemplate the construction of a mountain.*

To achieve shared perfection we must strengthen linkages between the focal points of our being. The body–mind linkage is strengthened when we have acquired and practice a clear system of values and pursue a rational approach to living. The spirit–mind linkage is fostered when we clarify our aspirations and develop our ability to understand concepts. The spirit–body linkage is promoted when we practice patience. Why patience? Because our aspirations and spiritual yearnings most often result in a sense of dissatisfaction with our physical circumstances. This dissatisfaction is interpreted as various needs at the level of the body. Patience is required to enable us to reappraise our needs and to help us live with our situation even as we aspire for something else.

MEDITATION AND PRAYER

In my own transformational journey, I have found prayer to be invaluable. By prayer, I do not mean pleading and petitioning the god of our ego-centered understanding. Rather, prayer as I understand it and as it has worked in my own life is a catharsis and a channeling.[4] It is a way for me to externalize my innermost feelings and experience myself in relation to a vaster level of existence. It is also a way for me to consecrate my entire being and recommit myself to Love, to openness, and to growth. I have often found that verbalizing my prayer brings me into an atmosphere of Reverence. Whenever I take a problem with me into prayer, I experience a distancing from the problem. I have had experiences in prayer where my sense of being would enlarge, making it impossible to speak. There are times also where my head would "disappear" such that I lost all sense of having a separate existence from our collective existence.

The God I pray to would not (and perhaps cannot) fulfill my desires or grant me advantages over my fellowmen. After all, my God is their God too! Even if I were to pray to God to grant me victory over my "enemies," it would be revealed to me that my "enemies" are only a matter of my perception. Prayer helps me to see that the only enemy I must be wary of is narrowness of being and a restrictive interpretation of what constitutes my self. In a way — at least, this is the way it has worked for me — prayer allows us to access directly the consciousness we aspire to in our meditation practice.

Notes, Chapter 6

1. This greater will is not to be identified with wielding power and force, but with our ability to align ourselves with higher principles.
2. The Higher Self designates that level of our being where our aspirations and the longing for a more meaningful life are generated.
3. This is not to say that there is anything wrong in being a tourist. However, when it comes to spiritual life, being a tourist amounts to nothing more than insincerity and pretense.
4. The kind of channeling I am talking about here is of the pure variety, i.e., without images, words, or thoughts.

7 Expressing Attitudes that Say "Yes" to Life

CREATING AND MAINTAINING SACRED SPACE

Transformation does not take place in a vacuum. It occurs when we substitute each of the innumerable "No's" with which we meet the events of life with a "Yes." Usually, we form an image of the life we desire and build a mental and emotional fortress to keep out what does not harmonize with our personal designs. It is necessary for the transformational process that we dismantle our fortresses and become open and receptive to the objective world of other people. If the ideal of transformation has any validity at all, it must express itself in enhanced relationships with the world outside of our heads.

The attitudes that we take with us into our interactions with the world determine how we experience the world. And since transformation is really a joint endeavor between us and higher levels of reality, proper attitudes clear a way for Divine Energies, just as assuredly as improper attitudes block them. Having proper attitudes is not the same as making or holding affirmations. By proper attitudes, we mean an inner posture toward life that will assist us in creating and maintaining a certain Sacred Space in our being. This Sacred Space represents freed energy that is not committed to a predetermined behavior routine.

The relationship between the attitudes with which we meet life and the freed energy, or Sacred Space, became one of my interests following an experience I had some years ago with this freed energy. This experience and the significance it held for me are described below.

A Personal Encounter with "Freed Energy"

One day in April 1977, I was driving to Toronto from Burlington, a city some thirty-five miles away. During my trip, I was stopped by a policeman for exceeding the speed limit. As he approached my car, I had the realization that here was an individual with the thankless task of saving the lives of people such as me by enforcing laws for the safe use of the road. I conceded within myself that this was a ticket well-deserved. When he handed me the ticket, I thanked him in all sincerity. At that moment, I experienced a sensation usually reserved for my most intensive meditation. My consciousness shifted to a higher level, and with this shift, my entire body became bathed in a light, refreshing sensation. It gave the feeling of weightlessness. I drove the rest of the way in this state to my destination.

The trip was otherwise uneventful except for the time I stopped at a traffic light on a Toronto street. As I waited for the light to change, I did so with the most profound patience. At that moment, time stood still. I had no thoughts, no concerns, no preoccupations. I was just "being there." If there was a period of my life when I was able to say *I Am* with more conviction than any other, this was it. That moment was so unassuming, so "unspecial" that that would have been the end of the matter were it not for something else that happened in relation to it that same day.

That incident occurred later that evening while I was back at my home in Burlington, sitting in bed, doing my meditation practice. During these earlier days of my meditation practice, I was accustomed to feeling distinct shifts in consciousness and bodily awareness, as if changing channels on a television set. Usually, I would not feel these coming. They would just happen and I would be left with the realization that something had changed. This time, after several such shifts, I had the full sensation of sitting in the car that day, at that very stoplight where I had the sensation of total emptiness before. This was not a memory of the event, as I had no sensation of being in bed. I was in my car! When I came out of the experience, I had the unmistakable sensation that I was back at that junction just moments before.

Taken in isolation, the impact on me might not have been as profound. I realized that the *I Am* experience of that day created a "window" for me to have the bodily experience later on. It was as if that moment was reserved for future use, not cluttered up with ego-centered concerns. An equivalent experience in ordinary life is when, in writing a sentence, I leave a space because I am not sure of the word I want to use. Later on, I can go back to fill in that missing word.

The succession of experiences, starting with my encounter with the policeman, taught me how important attitudes are for transformational work. For me, the entire episode began with an attitude that acknowledged my spiritual solidarity with the policeman. From that initial attitude I was able to experience for myself the relativity of time and space. Also, I learned that just as I was able to leave a "space" in my life for future use, I am currently able to do the same thing. The implication for transformational work is that we can retroactively change the meaning of an experience or give meaning where one is lacking. No matter what I experience, I alone, through my attitude, can determine the potential of this experience for good.

FACILITATING THE TRANSFORMATIONAL IMPULSE

If we return to the reproduction analogy in Chapter 1, we can compare the attitudes necessary for the facilitation of the transform-ational impulse to the dietary regime of a mother-to-be. The attitudes that are most critical for the facilitation of the impulse can be recognized as:

- Appreciating the wonder of Life by expressing gratitude for existence;

- Expressing true courage by removing the limits we impose on the Self;

- Expressing contentment by removing the mortgage we place on the Soul;

- Expressing love or compassion by striving always to perceive a process, such as a human being, from its own center of awareness;

- Taking responsibility for our own growth by being always willing to convert knowledge to understanding;

- Expressing true faith by being open to new possibilities;

- Expressing true humility by not being loath to share the ordinary fate of ordinary men and women.

Appreciating the Wonder of Life

The movement and expansion of consciousness in us is an incredible wonder. Every thought in us is literally a new avenue that consciousness can explore to take us into a totally new perception of the Universe and a new relationship to it. Every heartbeat carries with it a fresh mandate for the renewal of life.

Despite the wondrousness of all that is going on under the surface, we continue to be preoccupied with the surface action. We are mesmerized by our thoughts, like the movie viewer seeing familiar expressions of life on the screen, not realizing that it is only the slowness of our perceptual apparatus that makes us see a series of independent, self-contained pictures as dynamic, moving images. We forget that our thoughts about life and Life as it is are two different realities. We are caught up in the unconscious drama of laying personal claim to thoughts that intrude into our awareness, expressing them in feelings, words, and actions as if we are giving expression to the Life principle itself. We say such things as "I am angry," or "I am jealous," or "I am poor," or "I am afraid," on and on. We then accept our own perceptions as objective conditions of Life, as the constituent stuff of Life, missing the true Life, which, like the calm depths of the ocean, lies undisturbed by the surface ripples generated by air currents of thoughts.

We also take Life for granted, and the extent to which we do so is evidenced by the way we relate to the magical organ in us, the heart. We fail to see that what we perceive to be the continuous throb of life is really the alternating phases of personal life and death. There is never any guarantee that this last heartbeat will not be our final one, that the gap that comes between two heartbeats will not just extend into infinity. We need only to contemplate this to realize that we are debtors to Life.

Of all the attitudes that are critical for the transformational process, having an appreciation of the wonder of Life is paramount. Without this appreciation, it is virtually impossible for us to become alert to the opportunities for inner growth. In its relation to the process of expanding our consciousness, appreciating the wonder of Life is like lighting the pilot lamp of the heart. Just as the pilot lamp in a furnace makes it possible for the furnace to turn on under the appropriate conditions, a proper appreciation for the wondrousness of Life ensures that we are psychologically ready to participate in life in a contributive way when opportunities present themselves.

Another way in which an appreciation of the wonder of Life can assist us in our spiritual journey is in getting us to use our imagination positively. Each one of us has an awesome power to create our own individual reality. This power operates chiefly through our belief system. Whatever each of us is able to validate for ourselves and hold to be true must have already been regarded as a possibility in our individual systems of beliefs. Because we are normally unaware of this power, we use it unknowingly to torture ourselves through rigidities, fear, and other forms of psychological complexes. When we start to appreciate the wonder of Life, we take the first step in becoming conscious of the awesome power of our belief system to shape our reality as we experience it subjectively. At the same time, we also take the first step in using it to create a reality that is positive and Life-affirming.

Once we begin to sow the seeds for a positive, Life-affirming reality through an appreciation of Life, it won't be long before we realize that *all things are possible*. In our pilot lamp analogy, we can say that this is how we keep the pilot lamp of the heart lit, thereby keeping open the possibilities for improving our lot.

The awareness that all things are possible does not only mean mental acknowledgment, but full emotional rapport with this realization. We have to free the heart — the emotional, feeling, and desire nature — to roam unencumbered into the realms of possibilities. This is the manner in which we make contact with "higher order" realities. The heart is fully equipped to do so while the rationalizing intellect is not. It is only much later that the intellect is able to find a way to acknowledge and conceptually interpret to itself what is going on. The intellect with its concept-making powers is like the flame of the furnace. It comes into operation when all the conditions are right.

Should the pilot lamp of the heart not be lit, in the sense that we are unaware of possibilities for growth, it would be impossible to convince the intellect of even the most imposing and elementary aspects of reality. This phenomenon has been demonstrated time and time again when people in a more "primitive" culture demonstrate an inability to "see" things they have not previously comprehended or held to be possible. I once read somewhere that when Darwin's vessel neared the Galapagos Islands while on one of his famous investigative voyages, the inhabitants of those islands did not "see" his ship and therefore did not respond to its presence. They could not "see" it because they never thought that a ship of that size was possible.

It is also acknowledged in scientific circles that the "I will believe it when I see it" type of skepticism is much less conducive to scientific discoveries than a more open attitude represented by "I will see it when I believe it."

One of the contemplative practices that I engage in is to isolate and feel the heartbeat among the many sensations that compete with it for my attention. I then ponder the power source behind the beat of my heart and try to identify with it. This gives me a sense of Life as an independent agency flowing in and manifesting itself as me.

Removing the Limits We Impose on the Self

Next to having an appreciation of the wonder that is Life, removing limits and barriers that we impose on the Self is the most critical attitude for anyone to adopt who is concerned with giving longevity to the transformational impulse. We impose limits on the Self in thoughts, words, feelings, and attitudes. How often have we said, upon hearing of something unpleasant happening to someone else, "Oh, if that ever happens to me I won't be able to live through it. I'd die!" We do not realize that what we are doing in such circumstances is to presumptuously impose limits on the Self.

Whenever we set conditions on Life as in the above, whether through fear or pride, we are in fact letting the historical self dictate the terms of our lives. We are pushing the real Self, which knows no limits, into the backseat. *This is why we often have to face in real life the very things we most fear would happen to us.* It is as if this is the only way that the Self can convince the mind of its resilience and impress upon us that it does not relish the shackles we try to place upon it.

To remove these limits, we have to consciously confront, at a mental level, the things and events that we fear. In doing this, we usually find that the things we fear are not half as bad as the fear itself. As if to show how foolish we are to live in fear, the fear will invariably leave us when we can live out, in the mind, all the conditions that we thought we would not be able to survive. If we insist on being fearful, timid, and retreating from Life, we place the Self in the position of engineering situations to convince the mind that it is resilient and ought not to be placed in a mental straitjacket.

Clearly, the basis of our presumption in placing restrictions and conditions on Life is our inability to trust. Before we are able to shift to an attitude of openness we must have developed the capacity to trust. After all, if we cannot trust Life, who, or what can we trust? Where were we when the incredible drama of biological conception began? And did we know of ourselves how to be born? We mistrust Life because we want to feel personally in control of the various elements of Life. It is this desire for control, buttressed by mistrust, that causes us to impose limits and conditions on the expressions of Life.

I remember in my own life when I found it impossible to pray that God's will be done in my life. I found it impossible because I feared that God's will for my life could run counter to my plans for myself: "What if it's God's will that I should lose both my legs? What if it's God's will that I lose my sight? What if . . .?" What I was failing to realize is that there are people living and functioning without sight, or legs, and all the other myriad things I feared I would lose if I gave in to the design of Life for me. The design of Life is greater than our own individual designs, and ironically, it is only when we begin to acknowledge this that Life begins to trust itself to our care to a greater and greater degree.

Opening the Door of Contentment

It is one of the greatest fallacies of our time to think that our personal level of contentment lies in anything external to us. Because of societal and other conditioning, we have come to regard contentment as a conditional response: "If only I had so-and-so, I'd be content," we often tell ourselves. The so-and-so could be anything: the right amount of money, the right job, the right mate, the right car or house, and on and on. For anyone who has taken the time to look objectively at the average human being, nothing could be further from the truth. If an individual cannot be content where she is right now, she can never be content, because contentment is nothing more than a mental attitude, no less so than an attitude of gratitude, or kindness, or patience. We can change our level of contentment just as easily as we can change our attitude.

Once, during a meditation, I had an insight into the enigma of contentment. It occurred to me that contentment could be achieved by just opening a door inside myself and stepping through! I was also able to see that contentment is one of the keys to spiritual mastery and freedom. Because, in arriving at the place in ourselves where contentment resides, we have eliminated the need for all the preconditions that we usually impose on ourselves before allowing ourselves to feel contented.

Once in that inner place of contentment, we are much further ahead than those who seek money, power, and prestige as prior conditions of their own states of contentment. The millionaire, for instance, has to accumulate his fortune before he can feel contented; the tycoon has to amass an empire; the demigod has to cultivate and court devotion from his followers. By being in that place called contentment, we would "be" a millionaire ahead of the millionaire, a tycoon ahead of the tycoon, and many rungs ahead of the demigod. Actually, there is no guarantee that when the millionaire has accumulated his millions he will feel contented, or the tycoon his empire, or the demigod his following, for that matter. This is why contentment is such a prize.

When we are able to realize that contentment is a mental attitude, an emotional and mental door that we can open and step through, we get a sense of what it means to be spiritually free. We have succeeded in paying off the mortgage that had been placed on the Soul. We do indeed mortgage the Soul when we grant powers outside of ourselves authority over our internal level of contentment. We make that which has no master, save the One, subservient to time and a debtor to material things.

In terms of a daily practice, I would suggest that at the end of each day we take time to reflect on the difference we have made to the world by our activities. We should ask of ourselves, "Have I made the best use of my abilities and my position in the world?" We must then reflect on whether we are using our abilities just for material success, or whether we are applying ourselves in a way that makes a creative difference to the world, and consequently furthers our transformation.

As we do this exercise, we should try to imagine the place we individually occupy in the world being filled by someone else, particularly someone less privileged. How would this person feel about the position that he or she is temporarily occupying? How is that less privileged person functioning in your job? How contented is that person in that job? For those of us who are mothers, what if a childless woman occupied your place? How would she feel being the mother of your children, the wife to your husband?

These reflections helps us to sample our "places" in the world for their "objective contentment value." Usually, we do not realize the potential for contentment in our individual situations. By distancing ourselves for a while from our individual situations, we begin to see, little by little, that contentment does not lie in external situations, but in ourselves.

There is another side to this exercise. We may get insight as to whether we are in the position that is right for us. We may find that the position we occupy in the world may not need us, in the sense that any of a million people could be doing exactly what we are doing without there being a difference in the task being done. Sometimes we occupy positions in the world that do not give us the challenges and interactions we need for the exercise of the Soul. In such circumstances, we actually sell the Self short. And for what? A title? A bank account? How much is the Soul worth? Finally, what difference are we making to the world for actually having been here?

Expressing Love or Compassion through the Art of Listening

My working definition of love is this: to be able to perceive and experience a process from its own center. For me it is the most complete way that we can partake of the reality of another being, human or otherwise. In the case of human beings, we often hear that God dwells within each individual. But how do we relate to this piece of information when we have to deal directly with another person, particularly if that individual is being unpleasant to us? The solution lies in trying to place ourselves at that individual's center of awareness.

Each of us views the world from a certain space that is very primordial. That space is the self-love we each carry. When we talk about God dwelling within, it is in the form of each individual's self-love. For one to love the God in another is more than loving what is noble and upright in that person. Loving the noble and the upright is part of the story, but not all of it. To truly love someone we must love that person's self-love. And this is not easy. But it is only then that we are able to view the world from the space out of which that person also sees it.

When we learn to love the self-love of others, we know that we do not love them because they love us first. Also, the person who is loved at the level of his self-love receives an opportunity to expand his understanding of self. The person who loves in this way is saying, "I am with you. I am not against you. I believe that you only want what is good for yourself, and with that I am in agreement." When we genuinely approach others with such an attitude, they will normally have to let down their guard, because they sense that they do not have to defend themselves from an external threat. Eventually, they will find it possible to admit to the fact that we are all connected and not separate.

Our capacity to listen is also one measure of our capacity to love, because listening is a way of giving our attention to others and sharing in their reality. Listening is a first step in giving expression to the reality of our connectedness. It is also the first practical step in expressing empathy and love for one another. When we can express this degree of empathy we begin to see that each individual has a unique set of problems and challenges that he or she has to work at solving in order to fulfill Life's transformational agenda for him or her. A lack of willingness to share someone else's reality is a failure to love and a missed opportunity for us to expand our own being. For where else can we expand our being except in contact with the beings of others?

As a spiritual practice, listening is something we can do at all times, and it does not require any special time and place. I regard listening as a spiritual practice, because the ears represent the most under-utilized of our senses. Usually, we are so preoccupied with sending signals and making impressions that we effectively block out most incoming signals, even cries for help.

Listening, therefore, presents us with one of the best opportunities to experience the world objectively. Every other means of perception is so intertwined with our own mental images that what we perceive is usually a projection from our inner realities onto the outer environment. By making listening a conscious act, we will establish points of contact with the objective universe and thereby create doorways for ourselves out of our own subjectivity, our self-made cocoons.

Even when we begin to open up to the objective world by taking time out to listen, we may still block incoming images by our fascination with our own internal goings-on. How often has someone begun to tell us a personal experience when, without letting that individual finish, we proceed to tell of an experience of our own that we think might be similar? Rather than "being there" for that person, we compete for their attention. If we cannot listen and give ourselves the chance to sample someone else's reality, Life will find more arduous means for us to accomplish the same task.

Converting Knowledge to Understanding

One of the problems that initially besets us on the transformational path is that there seems to be so much to know, so much to assimilate, that it just doesn't seem possible that we can remember it all. We might feel afraid that a crucial datum of knowledge will be forgotten at a critical moment. How is the problem to be solved?

The solution lies in how we store the knowledge that we've acquired. If the knowledge is stored where it is easily accessible, then the problem is solved. This can be done by a series of minor transformations. First, the thought energy that is knowledge must be converted into emotional energy, which is understanding. When we understand, we are able to *feel* what we know, "stand under" it and wield that knowledge about. As a next step, the emotional energy, which understanding represents, must be converted into electrical energy. This is done when we live out the knowledge as best we can as we understand it. By this action, we create new nerve impulse pathways from the new knowledge. These new nerve impulse pathways create new habit patterns that, when reinforced by hormonal reactions, result in automatic body responses.

New habits and the hormonal and neurological responses that support them become the tangible outcome of acquiring knowledge. This is learning, and it is accumulated learning that constitutes experience. With experience, we do not have a problem trying to retrieve knowledge that is stored away somewhere in the brain because the knowledge has become a part of us — as intimately as our name. There is now no dichotomy between the knower and the known, for they are now one and the same. The problem of retrieving knowledge now disappears.

When knowledge is not converted to understanding, it can derail the quest for meaningfulness and the transformative work that we are hosting. There is a certain dynamic involved here, determined by the very paradoxical nature of knowledge itself. As we awaken spiritually, we acquire knowledge through the process of finding outer corroboration for inner truths. In our search for spiritual knowledge, we are in a similar situation to the developing child who constantly asks, "What is this? What is that?" The child already knows what it is that it is asking about, in the sense that it has already registered itself in consciousness. All the child needs is the rational assessment of the thing to make its knowledge complete. This inward knowing, then outward turning for confirmation, is what enables the mind of the child to grow.

It is this same process which enables the Soul to grow in the spiritual seeker. The spiritual seeker searches for outer representations of interior truths, but to confirm these truths requires more initiative than in the case of the child. If the seeker does not apply what is confirmed externally, he or she would, in effect, be discounting inner truth, his or her own inner reality. Consequently, he or she would be hemorrhaging spiritually. There is no doubt about it! The nature of this hemorrhage is loss of Will. And in the final analysis, our Will is our life.

The mechanism through which we might experience hemorrhaging of our Will is subtle and fascinating. When we set out on the path of spiritual discovery, the inner being is filled with psychic tension. This tension exists as a direct result of the many mysteries that capture our interest and imagination as we seek to plumb the depths of the Soul. As a mystery is solved to our satisfaction, it dissolves and we gain knowledge in return. As the mysteries that confront us are dissolved one by one, the tension in our inner being is lessened. But we must keep up our interest and its accompanying tension if we are to continue our search. To achieve this, we must replace that tension which is lost through a decrease in the number of mysteries with a new kind of tension that comes from the challenges of applying the newly acquired knowledge.

As a mystery is solved and psychic tension is exchanged for knowledge, unless we apply what is learned and develop understanding we will gain nothing, but rather lose ground. We become mentally flaccid, intellectually impotent. Our situation would then be like the old woman in the fairy tale *Aladdin's Lamp*, who exchanged the old, magical lamp for one that glitters but has no genie to respond to its owner's call.

Faith: The Power of Transcendence

Faith is, perhaps, one of the most talked about of spiritual virtues, and perhaps one of the least understood. It is also most crucial in our endeavor to embody and become a channel for Divine Energies. What really is faith? And how to we incorporate it in daily practices? Unfortunately, faith has almost become synonymous with belief in something. Faith has nothing to do with believing in anything. It is a level of attunement, a way of being. We get an insight of the true meaning of faith from one of the discourses of the apostle Paul on the subject. He said, "Faith is the substance of things hoped for, the evidence of things not seen." (Heb. 11:1) What Paul is touching upon here has more to do with physics than religion, as it is conventionally understood. He is really addressing the physics of relativity.

By saying that faith is the substance of things hoped for, Paul is implying that faith is synonymous with our power to live beyond imposed limitations. The substance of things hoped for is just another way of addressing our ability to experience a reality that we are aspiring for as if it already exists. This is the power of transcendence. In a practical way, it is our ability *to have* in deprivation, *to taste* in abstinence, *to be fulfilled* in need. It means that we are able to transcend time. Usually, time is that factor which stands between something we hope for and its actual manifestation. To live as if we are already in possession of that which we hope for is to live beyond time, to live transcendentally.

Also, by saying that faith is the evidence of things not seen, Paul is saying that faith is a way of knowing without the need for verification by the physical senses. To accept evidence for the existence of things not ascertainable by the senses is to live beyond the limitations of space. Just as one does not have to go physically to Paris to verify that the Eiffel Tower exists, or to London to verify the existence of the Tower of London, there are many aspects of Reality for which we do not need verification from the physical senses before we can accept their validity. The aspect of faith that we are dealing with here is intuition. This is intuition as a new faculty, which we can and must develop.

When we put these two aspects of faith together, we can say that faith is the power to live beyond time-space limitations, to live in the fourth dimension. We can now see why faith should be included among the repertoire of our daily practices. Faith is a way of exercising the new faculties that accompany our acquaintance with the higher planes of existence. In exercising these faculties we acclimate ourselves to the "supersensible" worlds. Faith is therefore a demonstration of confidence in the efficacy of the principles that we are trusting ourselves to; and it is in such demonstrations that these principles become firmly established in our life.

The Practice of Humility

In many religious traditions, humility is recognized as one of the essential virtues. The apostle Peter says: "God opposes the proud but gives grace to the humble." (1 Pet. 5:5) The Chinese sage Laotzu says: "When [a man] is humble he can grow."[1] Humility marks out a person for power, because the Powers of the Universe know that such an individual will not lord it over her fellows but use the resources at her disposal to assist in the facilitation of our collective transformation.

Since humility is so important, is there a practice that can instill humility? Is humility something detectable by outer appearance? One of my favorite spiritual stories concerns a disciple of one Sufi teacher who criticizes the teacher of an acquaintance for wearing fine clothes and not demonstrating outward signs of piety. The first disciple boasts that his own teacher is not like his acquaintance's, but wears the clothing of the poorest classes of people to show his humbleness of spirit. The second disciple replies, "If he is so humble why does he need to show it?"

If humility is not detectable by appearance, what then can be used as an indicator of the truly humble person? For me, the humble person is one who is not loath to share the ordinary fate of ordinary men and women. Thus, the humble person is one who lives and breathes solidarity with the spiritual aspirations of fellow human beings. When we are in a state of humility, we do not fear the unknown, for in doing so we would be placing more validity on what we have individually experienced than on the collective experiences of humanity. The humble person appropriates no such power unto himself or herself. To be humble is to be open, vulnerable, and very aware of the ephemerality of our existence as a separate ego and personality. When we are humble we learn to live every day as if it could be our last.

Humility is definitely a quality that we can practice and grow in. In some ways, its relationship to transformation is similar to what a foundation is to a house. By identifying ourselves with the experiences common to people in general, we create the conditions necessary to become a source through which collective human needs find fulfillment. In the context of the impersonal process that characterizes the expansion of consciousness, our humility makes it possible for the Life Process to use us as facilitators in the lives of others. It is possible for us to know what people need to help them grow when we, through spiritual solidarity, share their dilemmas and suffering.

Notes, Chapter 7

1. Witter Bynner (translator), *The Way of Life According to Laotzu* (New York: Capricorn Books, 1962), 69.

8　Beyond the Bondage of Polarity: Transmuting the Sexual Impulse

SEX AND TRANSFORMATION

When most spiritual seekers in the West think about the possibility of sex making a positive contribution to the transformation of consciousness, they usually think of the outer aspects of tantric practices that have migrated to the West from the East. Since most of the printed material available in the West seems to restrict itself to the demonstration of explicit sexual poses, many seekers get the idea that tantra promotes sexual license. Actually, participation in the outer form of sex mysteries without the subtle inner teachings does nothing for transformation. It amounts to nothing more than self-deception.

I encountered an example of this misdirected approach towards the role of sex in transformation during a visit I made to the Rajneesh ashram at Poona, India, in late 1978. I had included his ashram on the itinerary of my five-week tour of India because I wanted to personally observe what sort of expression his teachings were taking in the lives of his followers. I had read one of his books, *Meditation — The Art of Ecstasy*,[1] and was intrigued, to say the least. What he was saying resonated so much with some of my own experiences that I honestly felt that I could have written some parts of that book. I was especially taken in with the biographical sketch at the end of the book. In it, he said that he was not a guru, but also that he did not deny anyone's need to be a disciple. In his writings, he seems totally detached from the traditional role of the guru. This was what particularly enticed me to Poona.

As it usually happens when I travel, I seemed to find the right people who supplied me with the information that I needed. Just two hours after arriving at Poona, I made the acquaintance of a woman disciple from the United States while lunching at a restaurant. She turned out to be a very good contact because I learned from her a great deal about the goings-on at the ashram. It was quickly apparent to me that I had arrived with the wrong impression. For one, despite what I had read about him not regarding himself as a guru, Rajneesh was acting the part of the guru par excellence. Just like that, illusion number one was shattered. Furthermore, he ran a very tight ship, demanding absolute trust and loyalty from his followers. To become a disciple and beneficiary of his guidance, one had to be initiated into his group, wear an orange robe and a mala (a string of beads like a rosary with a cameo of Rajneesh), and receive a new name.

This strict external discipline seemed to be more than compensated for by the absence of the strict moral code that traditional gurus demand of their followers. For example, in contrast to many teachers who hold that sexual discipline or even abstinence is a necessary part of spiritual work, his followers were free to explore their sexual passions without inhibition.

This lack of inhibition about sexuality sometimes took on amusing, if not bizarre overtones. After just over an hour of conversation with my informer, she invited me back to her apartment to meet her live-in boyfriend. We were engaged in a three-way conversation for only a few minutes when she disappeared and returned in the nude to pick up her end of the conversation again. I surmised that she wanted to demonstrate the liberating effects her guru's teachings had on her by showing that she had no self-consciousness about her body. She mentioned, quite innocently, the several times she found the local Indian men gaping at her through drapeless windows as she took her daily "wind baths."

During the next couple of days I spent in Poona, it became obvious that despite what spiritual work might have been going on in the depths of these disciples' beings, on the surface sex was providing immediate compensation for their "troubles." I got the feeling that what most of them were after was love and acceptance from an authority figure, and "Bhagwan" — as Rajneesh was addressed by his disciples — did cut a fine authority figure indeed.

I left Poona with a burdened heart for these *sanyassins* (as he called his disciples) and a resolve to determine in my own mind what place sex can constructively assume in an individual's unfolding.

THE SPIRITUAL PSYCHOLOGY OF SEX

Much of the context within which the psychology of sex is studied owes its origin to the repression ideas of Freud. So pervasive is his influence that these ideas have infiltrated the understanding of many of us concerned with the transformational process. For example, I once heard a yoga teacher tell a yoga class that it is dangerous for them to repress their sexual desires, and that the best time for spiritual work is when they are older and no longer under the compulsion of their biological urges. The impression was given that all abstinence is repression. At the time, this piece of advice seemed to me to be equivalent to telling a motorist that the best time to start a long journey is when the gasoline in the tank has been used up.

To understand the spiritual psychology of sex, we must break sex down into its two separate and apparently unrelated functions. These are the biological or reproductive function, and the psychological or pleasure function. The biological or reproductive aspect is easy to understand, and it is with the psychological or pleasure aspect that we seem to have the most problems. This is because the relationship between these two functions can be missed. At first glance, it seems as if the pleasure aspect of sex is an afterthought of Nature — as the way for Nature to guarantee that species multiply, a sort of enticement, if you will. However, on deeper examination, it appears to be the other way around, with reproduction being added to the pleasure aspect for a "free ride."

The pleasure aspect of sex is a way for individuals to have access to levels of consciousness that are not readily accessible in the ordinary waking state. Thus the energies available through the sex function serve as a corrective for the stranglehold our individualistic and separative tendencies place on our psychic energy. The sex impulse brings people together so that they can lose their separativeness. The function that sex provides, psychologically speaking, can be seen as a "thawing out" of the individual at the ego level to make him or her more cooperative. So effective is this thawing out process that many, many promises are made by sex partners, which they are incapable of keeping afterwards. What is recognized as the sex drive (at least, in men) can usually be correlated with the level of egotistic ambition and the drive for power. It is as if an exaggerated power complex must be counter-balanced by the need for total acceptance by another.

The psychology behind this expression of sex is so subtle that the best I can do to communicate it is by way of the following parable.

> A nobleman of great wealth had a son, who, in a fit of pride, left his father's home to make a name for himself. He was frustrated that he had to depend on his father for his livelihood and thus sought to establish himself on his own merit. Not quite understanding the extent of his father's influence, he was even more frustrated in his effort to live on his own and establish his independence because the local residents bestowed favors upon him when they found out who he was.
>
> He was quite annoyed by all this, for he wanted to be recognized on his own merit, not on his father's. Unable to make a living on his own, he took to returning to his father's house at night to steal. Servants reported the thefts to the nobleman, but he, suspecting his son to be the thief, instructed the servants to make it even easier for him. They were to leave windows unlatched and valuables unattended and unsecured. Through this act of complicity on the part of the father, the son was able to make a living without the feeling that he had to accept his father's charity.

In our parable, the nobleman's son represents the ego that has left the totality of Being to establish itself on its own terms. It has chosen to become polarized and specialized. But since it is possible to drift from the Source of Being only for finite durations, it needs to tap back into this Source for sustenance. That is why we find that the stronger the ego or the separative drive, the stronger the sex impulse. On the other hand, the individual who does not drift too far from Source, who is not too caught up in his or her own separateness, is not possessed with the sex impulse to the same degree.

The paradox of sex is that one experiencing the impulse does not see it as a return to Source, but as an expression of individuality, an expression of his or her own "specialness." In reality, however, this impulse is a death-wish of sorts, and its consummation ends in a mini-death. Sex provides one with the experience of dying without the need to shed the body.

Sex and Spiritual Striving

Sex can become a problem in the transformational quest. It can become a psychological and biological hindrance to spiritual striving. Although I realize there are many views to the contrary, I say this without apology. Whether it becomes a problem, though, depends on where one is at in his or her development.

The difference between sex and other actions is that, contrary to every other form of action, when one engages in the sex act, one is risking everything one is — body, mind, and spirit. After each sexual encounter, one becomes emotionally drained and must start again from scratch to fill the being, to gather one's emotional energies into an effective force. When this energy is again organized, it is again emptied. This type of response to sex is one that punctuates the life with predetermined peaks of striving and fulfillment. The consequence is that one is locked into a narrow range of emotional highs and lows defined by these peaks and troughs of the sexual desire cycle.

Before we can make lasting gains in transformation, we have to break out of this narrow band that dictates our consciousness. We must move much further apart the pegs that mark the high and low tide lines of our emotional life. Our biopsychic organism must be attuned to a new rhythm with a much longer cycle and higher ranges than those determined by sexual tension and release. Breaking out of this sexually prescribed desire-fulfillment orbit is similar to launching a rocket. When a rocket is launched, its engine must generate sufficient thrust to take it away from the influence of the gravitational pull of the earth. But once outside this influence it can propel its way with very little expenditure of energy.

We can take two approaches as we try to attune our being to a longer cycle of striving and fulfillment. The first is abstinence, either complete or partial, and the second is by meeting the problem in a frontal attack. It is the frontal attack that is called tantra, which some Eastern traditions espouse.

Abstinence and celibacy help the individual endeavoring to evolve spiritually by ensuring that the urge for spiritual unity is not dissipated at an emotional and physical level. The psychological mechanism through which this is effected is quite straightforward. Spiritual development implies growth toward more openness and unity with others. If this openness and desire for union is expressed sexually, it leads to a reinforcement of our sense of separateness so that we go two steps back for every one forward, psychologically speaking.

Another reason why one may have to control sexual expression is that sex also reinforces Nature's preemptive access to human energy. This preemptive access fulfills our basic survival needs by giving priority to the production of various tissues and substances in the body. In this scheme, cells and substances necessary for reproduction rank ahead of other tissues. Substances for the brain and nervous system are next in priority, and so on, down the line. In this system of priorities, there has to be a trade-off between the protein molecules that build the body and those that go into the reproductive function. This means that every gram of reproductive substance generated by the body represents a loss to the next level in the chain of priority. It is easy to see how the brain and other vital systems can suffer when sexuality continues to have the highest priority in our life.

One school of thought suggests that the transformation of consciousness requires the brain to develop the ability to process additional and subtle levels of information that become available as our consciousness becomes transformed. Consequently, if we are not master of the sex impulse and its consummation, there is a net loss to the brain. Capitulation to the sex urge is thus a vote for the slow crawl implicit in Nature's evolutionary program as opposed to the rapid advance possible through the transmutation of energies.

Social factors also play a part in the need for sexual restraint. As we unfold, the sexual mores that keep sexual liaisons in check erode. For instance, the individual whose approach to life is primarily determined by cultural, social, and economic class, may contemplate sexual encounters only with others of the same group. In addition, one might seek out a mate who conforms to predetermined demographic, social, economic, and physical characteristics. Since spiritual transformation opens us up, these barriers begin to fall away, and we become more accommodating in our feelings and attitudes towards others. In a transformational mode of consciousness, possibilities for sexual liaisons are increased. Consequently, these greater possibilities must be counteracted by a lower emphasis being given to sexual activity.

Rehabilitating the Sex Impulse

There is a psychological principle which gives validity to the general idea that certain tantric practices can help one in the quest to transform consciousness. This general principle is that of apperception, our ability to experience ourselves experiencing. When we are able to insert a wedge of consciousness between a stimulus and the response that might automatically result from it, we can fulfill the need for action, which a stimulus calls for, with a certain level of detachment.

Specifically with regard to sex, if we are able to replace the desire for self-gratification (which so much characterizes expressions of sexuality) with a genuine desire for union, or a need to express love, then we create the opportunity to break free of the unconscious pull sexual attraction may have over us. At a psychological level, tantra works by taking a preoccupying desire to its fulfillment — but fulfillment with a difference. The difference is that by giving in to the action required by the preoccupation, we do so with all the being. Here we encounter another paradox of the transformational journey. When we give ourselves over completely to an act, we are able to elevate ourselves above the absurdity of being in bondage to an automatic stimulus-response pattern.

At this point we will consider the true experience of one individual who, without any prior knowledge of tantra or other magical sex rites, was able to experience the freedom-giving, transformation-enhancing role of sex in life. This individual was interviewed for this book and has permitted his story to be told in the hope that its experiential nature will ground our discussion of sex and transformation. The interview format has been retained to preserve the experiential and personal nature of the insights this individual is sharing with us.

BEYOND THE BONDAGE OF POLARITY: AN INTERVIEW

Question: *On the basis of your experience, what do you understand by the concept of tantra as it applies to sexuality?*

Answer: My own experience has shown me that between a man and a woman the opportunity is greatest for two human beings to experience unity of soul and will. Since as individuals, we are all physically separate, locked away from each other in a separate body, sex provides us with a window of escape from our separateness. If we use this window for the purpose for which it was designed, we would be able to attain to a higher level of being where we no longer automatically devote the bulk of our energy to the pursuit of self-gratification, but rather use it to become clear as to what higher purpose to which we should dedicate our lives. I believe that tantra is a window through which we can escape from our illusion of separateness.

Question: *Could you be a bit more specific?*

Answer: Well, as a result of my own experience, I have become convinced that the sex act between a man and a woman is to be no less than a holy sacrament and not something to be indulged in for purely selfish gratification. If the man approaches this act primarily out of a desire for his mate's happiness, striving to place her enjoyment ahead of his, and she likewise surrendering to him, then the way is open for both to become as one and to respond as one.

Question: *Can you tell us what teachings have influenced your attitude in these matters?*

Answer: Before having direct personal experience in this area, my attitude on sexual matters was shaped primarily by my high regard for certain biblical instructions. Foremost among these is the exhortation in the epistle of Paul to the Ephesians that ". . . men [ought] to love their wives as their own bodies. He that loveth his wife loveth himself," and ". . . a man [shall] leave his father and mother, and shall be joined unto his wife, and they two shall be one flesh. This is a great mystery . . . [So] let everyone of you in particular so love his wife even as himself; and the wife see that she reverence her husband" (Eph. 5: 27–33). I took these instructions to mean that there was a Mystery in the union of man and woman that went far, far beyond the urge or the perceived need for sensual gratification. I saw this exhortation that a man should love his wife "as his own body" as a great challenge.

The apostle Peter also made a connection between a man's love for his wife and his access to Divine blessings. He said that husbands should love their wives ". . . as being heirs together of the grace of life; that your prayers be not hindered" (I Peter 3:17). I felt that Peter gave away a bit more of the Mystery here by saying that husbands and wives are "heirs together" of the "grace of life." I asked myself: "Why specifically husbands and wives?" The answer that occurred to me is that husbands and wives have the potential to form the closest ties of any other two-person combinations. I believe they represent the shortest path possible out of individual human separateness.

Question: *How about this experience you've alluded to; can you tell us something about it?*

Answer: As for the experience itself, it had its roots in a long and loving relationship. I had been married for several years, and during this time I grew to love my wife very much. The more I grew to love her, the more exhilarating and emotionally fulfilling our lovemaking became. We approached this as something very special and took great care not to overindulge, sometimes waiting for long periods between encounters, just to keep the magic alive. Despite my happiness with my wife, something was missing. I felt that no matter how much I loved her, this love could never find complete expression in the sex act. I deeply longed for a more complete unity that would somehow transcend the enclosure of the body.

Mine was a heart calling out for a more complete expression of my love and unity in spirit with another human being, and one memorable day, this call was answered. During our lovemaking, my wife began to experience an orgasm of unusual strength. As usual, my happiness at her "success" knew no bounds, and as I held her ever more closely to me, the most unusual thing happened. A surge of "current" emanated from her body into mine, traveling through my organ to the base of my spine, then all the way to the forehead. With this occurrence, I experienced the most refreshing, soothing, and exhilarating sensation. It flowed down all over my body, even to my toes. I could find nothing to compare it to other than the sensation one gets from taking a refreshing, cool shower after vigorous exercise on some hot, humid, summer day.

The most remarkable thing about this experience was that it was not my usual climax, differing in many respects from it. For one, there was no emission of body substance. For another, this was not a physical sensation of pleasure, but one that was light and airy and full of energy. It did not make me feel spent and lethargic as a normal male climax would. And for the very first time, I fully understood why my wife was her most energetic after our lovemaking while I had to summon my deepest affection for her not to fall asleep afterwards.

Question: *I don't mean to discount the significance of this experience for you, but what sort of spiritual significance can you attribute to it?*

Answer: The spiritual significance of this experience is that we
had succeeded in sharing a common reality at a moment
when most people express their most distinctive traits.
We had literally become "one" as the apostle Paul
promised. As for me, I had become part of her reality,
had experienced a purely emotional orgasm, *her* orgasm.
We had truly become one flesh! That, to me, is a spiritual
experience. It was an experience of objective union.

Also, I felt that my life took a special turn with this
experience since it was the first of many more to come.
These other experiences were on other levels of being,
physical, mental, spiritual. I classify this one as being
on an emotional level. With all these experiences my
interest in transformational matters took on a new
vigor, and I have never looked back.

Question: *How easy do you think it is for others to have this
experience?*

Answer: I believe that if we can enter into the sex act with all of
our awareness, this experience is possible. We must
enter the sexual relationship with the purpose of
sharing in a joint experience, not to exploit, or to
conquer, and we must dedicate all of our being to this
aspiration. Sex then becomes more than a biological
function, but a sacrament. One does not enter into a
sacrament with part of oneself, but all of oneself. With
sex, it is only when more than the physical body is
committed to the act that our possibilities for transformation are awakened. With only the physical body
entering the act, sex is nothing more than a simple
stimulus-response exercise. But with the emotions,
mind, and will participating, it becomes a way for us
to call upon the force of consciousness to participate in
the act with us. This way, biological urge becomes
transmuted into a spiritual urge.

If I might make just one final comment, I would like
to say that experiences of this nature prove that whatever
presents itself as an obstacle on the path of transformation can become, with the right attitude, a stepping

stone. It is not a matter of technique, but of attitude. I did not know anything of technique or the existence of such an experience, and it found me. No matter how much technique we might apply, if the right attitude is lacking, we will not derive any benefit. The real "sex magic" is when we are able to buy out Nature's prior contract on our energy. This happens when we are able to harness sex, a function that is the clearest focus for most of our feelings of duality, to transcend duality. I believe that what we recognize as tantra in Eastern systems must have begun as a therapy to help people wean themselves from the bondage of polarity.

WOMEN AND TANTRA

Unfortunately, I am not aware of any information that addresses how the woman benefits from tantric practices. It seems that ancient rites were concerned with the problem of the male, not the female. This does not mean that women are treated as objects in tantra. It is just that their help comes from different quarters. If the sexual relationship takes place in the context of a long-term, caring commitment, the deeper psychic energies in the woman are awakened and brought to the fore. This relationship is symbiotic. It is a widely held esoteric principle that men and women are alternately positive and receptive in electromagnetic polarity with respect to their several "bodies." For example the *physical* body of the male is positive while that of the female is receptive in polarity. Next, we have positive polarity in the *etheric* body of the female and receptive in the male. At the next level, which is the *astral*, the male is again positive and the female receptive. The next level, the *mental*, finds the female with a positive polarity and a receptive one for the male. Again, at the level of the *causal* body, we find the male positive and the female receptive.

Sexual relationship deals with the etheric body, which regulates the life impulse and is the energy preform to the physical body. It is here that the female has a greater advantage over the male and that the psychic energies related to sexuality can be harnessed. This may explain why sexuality with respect to the female is less singularly focused on any one function or activity. It is more diffused, a fact which sexologists and psychologists see borne out by the greater abundance and diffusion of so-called erogenous zones in the body of the female. Sex is therefore more a matter of psychological atmosphere than biology. With the male, the biological aspect is more prominent. Tantra, therefore, works for the female when the male is able to recognize the importance of psychological ambiance. It is by feeding her self-esteem and confidence and by assuaging her anxieties that the male helps the female to strengthen her astral body, which in the male is positive. These reciprocal actions of the man on the woman's physical and astral bodies and the woman on the man's etheric and mental bodies help each other in becoming more rounded, more whole.

STEPS TOWARD TRANSMUTING THE SEXUAL IMPULSE

Ours is a civilization in which sex has taken on an exaggerated importance. Our whole economy relies on the manipulation of sexual desire in individuals as its chief marketing device. Within this cultural climate, the individual who wants to transmute the sexual impulse into higher energies faces a formidable task. Even when we turn to our religions, we find little help; we are offered mostly dogma, platitudes, and hypocrisy.

There are two basic approaches available to the spiritual seeker who wants to become master of the sex impulse. The first consists of running away from sexual temptations. This has been used for hundreds of years by nuns and monks of various traditions. This is not a feasible solution for the majority of us, and moreover, it doesn't work. It focuses too much on the problem and as a consequence empowers it. When this approach is taken, sex becomes as menacing and invincible as the seven-headed hydra of Greek mythology.

This brings us to the second approach. It calls for us to put sex into perspective among the other joys that life has to offer. The idea is not to focus on giving up anything, but to evaluate our life to make sure that we aren't selling ourselves short. We sometimes forget that sex is a means to an end and forget that there are other ways to get to that end result besides sex. As Ram Dass said so well in his response to a question on how one can deal with sexual desire: "The game is just to go into the reality where sex is like rubbing sticks together to make a fire. You get to the point where you're already existing in that place you were having sex to get to."[2] First of all, when relationship is placed ahead of sex, sex becomes honored as something that happens between two people, not something that one body does to another person's body. As Germaine Greer points out, one doesn't make love to a part of the body, but to another person. Once this lesson is learned, we will have taken a substantial step in transmuting the sexual impulse. The physical act of sex must be seen as the last act in a series of unions beginning at the spiritual level, then extending to the mental, emotional, and finally the physical.

Patience is a vital ingredient in getting to know another person and building a relationship with that person. When an attraction occurs, we need not work at suppressing it, but can instead do a series of checks: Do I know this person well enough? What are his or her goals and aspirations? How can I help this person fulfill his or her goals and aspirations? Can I teach this person anything, or is there something I want to learn from this person? Is this a person I can commit myself to on a long-term basis? It is possible that if we take the time to do this check as honestly as we can, we will begin to relate to someone of the opposite sex as a person and not just as the possessor of a sexual organ.

Another step we can take as we attempt to transmute the sexual impulse is to consider that there exist states of being much higher, much more ecstatic and fulfilling than sexual union. Several years ago, when I underwent the experience of an aroused kundalini, the ecstasy of that experience was so pronounced that one of my responses was: "With this available, who needs sex?" I am not suggesting that we seek out mystical experiences to satisfy our need for pleasure. It is sufficient to know that there are higher ecstasies possible than that available through sex. Jacob Needleman puts the matter into perspective with the insight that ". . . the whole corruption of religion, and therefore civilization, begins when the work of self-knowledge becomes subjectively less interesting than sexual fulfillment."[3]

Unfortunately, because we experience fragmentation in our beings we often feel incomplete in ourselves. Sex then provides a way for complementary parts to become reunited and therefore becomes the highest form of ecstasy that many of us have ever experienced. Because of this dynamic, we get the impression that we cannot live or function without the physical expression of sex. But the truth of the matter is that this depends on the extent to which men and women project aspects of their own beings onto each other.

In a state of fragmentation, each gender develops some aspects of the personality at the expense of others. It is mostly the need to experience these missing aspects that is felt as sexual attraction. However, when we begin to experience wholeness in ourselves, the strength of sexual attraction is attenuated. It stands to reason that many of the spiritual practices which help to recirculate energy in the body and help promote wholeness also help in the transmutation of the sexual impulse. Here I am speaking of Hatha Yoga, Tai Chi, sports done in moderation, massage, and meditation.

Finally, the cultivation of friendship between men and women, based on various interests, helps each gender to understand and appreciate the other as whole persons. Such interactions will help the male retrieve some of the projections he has placed on the female, and vice versa for the female.

Notes, Chapter 8

1. Bhagwan Shree Rajneesh, *Meditation: The Art of Ecstasy* (New York: Harper & Row, 1976).
2. Ram Dass, *Grist for the Mill* (Santa Cruz, Ca.: Unity Press, 1977), 109.
3. Jacob Needleman, *Lost Christianity — A Journey of Rediscovery to the Center of Christian Experience* (New York: Bantam Books, 1982), 58.

9   Catalysts and Distant Lights: The Role of Spiritual Teachers

THE NECESSITY OF TEACHERS

In some situations, the spiritual seeker may feel the need for the direction and guidance of a spiritual teacher. He may be at a loss as to how to go about finding the right person to fit this function since this task may present him with the dilemma of having to evaluate someone who could possibly be expressing Life at a higher frequency than he is. However, if the seeker is sincere in his spiritual seeking, he should not have too many problems finding someone to help him along on the journey.

When the seeker is insincere in his spiritual seeking, his search will in reality be for a teacher who embodies in the flesh the spiritual ideals he already holds for himself. Consequently, there should be no danger of the sincere seeker falling under the spell of a "false teacher," since it is the seeker who projects upon others the role of teacher. If the seeker has fallen under the spell of a "false teacher," it is only because he is not sincere enough in his seeking. Lack of sincerity occurs when we are greedy for knowledge and power and neglect to put the knowledge already gained into practice.

CHARACTERISTICS OF THE SPIRITUAL TEACHER

Teachers are mediators between the higher states of consciousness that are the goals of spiritual seeking and human aspirations. The teacher's task is to assist an individual to raise her aspirations to a level at which she is able to propel herself by her own efforts. The teacher also helps her understand her experiences so that she is able to use them to facilitate her own spiritual growth. The teacher, therefore, becomes an external standard by which the seeker can measure herself. But this does not mean that the teacher encourages one to seek answers through him. He points the way, and if he is truly successful in his work, he would succeed in getting the seeker to go beyond him.

The role of the spiritual teacher is a natural one, as it is a fulfillment of one of the principles that contribute to the harmonious functioning of the Universe. The teacher's role is one of service: He or she is at the service of the Universe to disseminate the achievements that have been made at the highest levels. The harmonious functioning of life requires that each time someone attains a certain degree of spiritual realization, he or she must feed the proceeds of that realization back into life so that the overall momentum in the Universe towards a collective realization is maintained. This process of individual attainment and voluntary reaching out with the entire being to facilitate the spiritual realization of others is not a flamboyant gesture or an unnecessary attempt to impress. When we become conscious in the higher realms, we are aware of humanity's spiritual needs on a scale commensurate with the breadth and depth of the consciousness we have attained. Wherever spiritual needs are detected, the being of the teacher (or his lifeblood) must flow out to nourish and facilitate the fulfillment required by this need. Generally speaking, whatever constitutes the sphere of our concerns becomes our body, and the size of our body delineates our consciousness. Thus, someone who possesses spiritual consciousness becomes a teacher by virtue of allowing his being, or lifeblood, to flow through the Cosmos, feeding and nourishing it. I believe when Christian theology talks about the blood of Christ washing away our sins, it is addressing something similar.

"GRADES" OF TEACHERS

We can find various "grades" of spiritual teachers around us, ranging all the way from the *Avatar* or the Savior, to the Savant or the Messenger. The Avatar or the Savior usually has an appeal that is more or less Universal in his or her ability to resonate with the spiritual needs of people regardless of their local religious traditions. The Savant or the Messenger, on the other hand, may have a local mission and may have a teaching characteristic of a time and place. As such, his sphere of influence may be small. In these respects, Avatars and Savants can be regarded as "catalysts" and "distant lights," with the role of "catalyst" fitting the Avatar more and that of "distant light" being more appropriate to the Savant. However, both categories of spiritual teachers may embody either role in varying degrees.

In the role of "distant light," a spiritual teacher facilitates the expansion of an individual's consciousness by delivering a certain message or teaching for humanity. This message may be presented in terms of a verbal teaching, and as such, its real value is in sowing visions in the human mind. The verbal aspect of a teacher's message is only the beginning of a series of instructions a seeker may require to lead him or her to spiritual clarity and eventual Realization.

The spiritual teacher acting in the role of catalyst enables the spiritual seeker to benefit from another level of contact. Functioning in this role, the teacher may also deliver his teaching in highly symbolic language. This ensures that the message satisfies many different levels of seekers and second, that it takes on a deepening meaning in our understanding as our experience grows and as our personal efforts at applying the teaching increase. Consequently, when a teaching message is first offered, there may be a great degree of variation in the interpretation individuals give to it. Some people may profess to understand while others may admit total confusion. Even among those who claim to understand, we might find varying interpretations. The word symbols that constitute a teaching combine with personal effort and under-standing to generate a process of growth through iteration. This growth process continues until the symbol is fully absorbed in our consciousness and disappears as a separate reality. This process of absorption is similar to that of an organic enzyme, which triggers certain chemical reactions, and, in the end, becomes itself part of the end product.

When a symbol becomes embedded in our consciousness, it

gives us additional tools with which to "see" Reality. As our seeing improves, the depth and clarity of our experiences also increase. In turn, our understanding and appreciation of the symbol are further enhanced. The entire process then begins anew. When this process of sublimation continues for a sufficient number of times, we learn to recognize in ourselves the characteristics we initially saw in the symbol. In this regard, we rediscover the teacher within ourselves, and realize that the teacher outside who focalized our deeper spiritual sentiments and spurred us on in the development of spiritual consciousness within ourselves was, in many respects, a projection from our own internal teacher to another on the outside. This is why sincerity is so important in our spiritual seeking, for it is our inner need that determines the characteristics of the teacher we seek. To the extent that we are genuinely seeking to fill a spiritual need, the qualities we seek out in a teacher will be those that will directly address these needs.

Necessary Qualifications of a Spiritual Teacher

To fulfill this most difficult task of planting messages that will expand as the spiritual seeker grows in understanding, teachers of the highest qualifications are needed. The teacher must be capable of establishing a set of contact points with the seeker so that his transformation can be facilitated all along the way to spiritual Realization.

The teacher must be capable of teaching on multiple levels. In addition to her words, she must present the seeker with a working model of what she encapsulates in her teaching. For example, it would be impossible for her to talk of peace on the outer level with any degree of sincerity without being a model of contentment on the inner one. The teacher must also satisfy the additional conditions outlined below:

- She must have two standards, one quite liberal for her followers, and a stricter one for herself.

- She must provide a way of escape that frees the seeker from points of view. The seeker must be encouraged to strive to outgrow the teacher.

- Her teachings will take on a particular emphasis depending strictly on which of humanity's many needs she identifies with.

First Point of Contact

The first contact point is established by the act of the teacher taking on the three-dimensional characteristics of a Divine Principle and living them out in time and space. He condenses himself so that he becomes understandable. He reaches people where they are, so he most often uses words and images even though he represents a reality that is beyond words and images.

The teacher might decide to fashion a teaching through a process that consists of several stages: First, he tunes in to the Cosmos with his own being. Second, he "audits" the stage of our collective human development and compares that against the spectrum of our potential. This gives him an idea of what our collective spiritual needs are. Third, he brings these needs to a mental focus in the form of pertinent questions concerning what is required to get us to take the next step in our evolutionary journey. Fourth, he uses his knowledge of the next step that we must take to infuse us with a new vision.

The teacher therefore bridges and lives in two worlds, the spiritual world of principles and the temporal world of restrictions. In squeezing an unfettered and multidimensional quality such as a Divine Principle into its three-dimensional counterpart, there may be a great deal of pain. This pain may come from being rejected and misunderstood and from frustrations at our human propensity to distort a teaching and ignore the invitation it contains.

There is a common misconception that teachers necessarily have to be demonstrably joyous. Actually, there is every reason why the opposite is the case. They can be persons of deep sorrow and grief. The sorrow and grief are bittersweet, because teachers also see life from a higher perspective and know that there is ultimately nothing to be sorrowful about. In the meantime, the teacher feels the grief that comes from his deep realization of how aimlessly the majority of us conduct our lives, missing valuable opportunities to awake to the wonder and miracle that is Life. The ordinary human mind assumes that teachers must live in bliss in the same way it misinterprets the act of generosity as a sign of abundance or the state of contentment as a sign of satiation.

Second Point of Contact

The second point of contact makes it possible for the teacher to transmit all that can be communicated at the verbal level. This is the most critical stage of the teacher's work, and its purpose is to demonstrate to all those willing to progress how the teaching expresses itself in the life of the teacher himself.

Because of the critical importance of this second point of contact, only those messengers who have had a historical existence and whose messages have been propounded during the course of their physical lives are qualified. This criterion is necessary for the reason that all teachings with transformative power must be fashioned from the Universal Consciousness and focused through the love, intelligence, and will of the person delivering it. In order for someone to bring a teaching that is relevant to the human situation, he must become thoroughly familiar with the needs of humanity at a specific level of our development. Such a familiarity is an essential criterion in making a teaching relevant to those to whom it is communicated, and it is a quality acquired only through the teacher's personal involvement in life.[1]

The teacher's life forms a crucial link in the chain toward higher consciousness. In order for the seeker to see a working model of a teaching or the effect of his teacher's fully transmitted teachings, he needs to turn his outer and inner eyes to the one who has brought him the teaching. Only then can he see the full potential of a message or system for bringing about changes in personal existence. For example, if there were elements in the teaching that could not be parceled out without becoming half-truths and lifeless platitudes, then the life of the one who carries the teaching must show what the teaching can do under conditions of perfect transmission. This requirement is so important that even in the case of an authentic teacher, distortions occasionally creep into his teaching when it is transmitted in written or verbal form after his departure. By then, the context of the teaching is lost, and its full impact severely muffled.

When there is full synchronization between the life of the teacher and his teaching, the seeker is able to make direct contact with a Divine Principle. However, even if he has done all that is required of him in living up to the principle taught by his teacher, the seeker would still not be complete in his instructions, because up to this point, the principle is still external to his nature. Until he can exude the principle from his innermost being, his training is not over. By the time he is able to do this, he will have arrived at the source of his teacher's teaching, to the very consciousness from which the teacher's message came forth. Actually, he will have merged with the teacher himself, and in a succeeding phase will go beyond the teacher.

The second point of contact ensures that a bridge is created by which the seeker can cross the abyss that separates the intellectual aspects of a teaching and its deep inner aspects. This is why great confusion can occur in the life of a seeker if the teacher sends him double signals. When there is a double standard, a split between what is being said and what is being done, it is evidence that the teacher is not operating from the core of the principle he claims to represent. Double standards sometimes indicate that the teacher may be an imposter and a charlatan.[2] These types usurp the role of spiritual teacher because they think that there is glamour in this function. It is against this type that Jesus' warning applies: "Beware of false prophets, who come to you in sheep's clothing but inwardly, are ravenous wolves. You will know them by their fruits." (Matt. 7:15) The seriousness of this warning cannot be overemphasized, for false teachers and false prophets are false not only on account of what they verbally teach, but also by their inability to apply those same teachings to their own beings. Because of this lack, the students of false teachers are denied the higher levels of contact, and thus opportunities for creating higher faculties are lost to them.

Were a student to encounter such inconsistences in a teacher, it is an indication that he has outgrown the one he has esteemed as teacher, and should move one. To stay would only result in frustration of his aspirations and a retardation of his growth. The subtle instructions needed to bridge the gap between intellect and direct experience can only come from his awareness of the teacher's unity with what he verbally teaches.

Third Point of Contact

The third point of contact is at the level of the Soul. Here the spiritual seeker is encouraged to develop her own internal guidance system, and the teacher shifts her concern for the seeker to her ability to break free. This shift is in fulfillment of one of the principles of spiritual growth. The individual is to be given less help so that through her own independent effort and will, she adds something new to our collective understanding about the subtleties and complexities of spiritual striving and realization.

The teacher, therefore, encourages her student to outdo and outgrow her. On this score, Jesus said to his disciples, "He who believes in me will also do the works that I do; and greater works than these will he do, because I go to the Father." (John 14:12) Here Jesus was providing his disciples with the incentive to reach into their own beings to carry the process of awakening and realization a bit further. Actually, if the mission of the teacher is successful, it would be impossible for her students not to go beyond her. For, in following the message she gave, they would have fully absorbed into their beings the principle of which the teacher was just a vehicle. In this sense, they would have fully assimilated the teacher such that her entire teaching would now have become an attitude, or a certain psychological stance, or a certain mental or emotional space, or still yet, an inner voice. Through their assimilation of the teacher's message, the teacher continues to live and work as a part of their own inner beings. Thus, this stage ends with the birth of a new faculty, the teacher being the recipe and an ingredient in the process.

Final Point of Contact

The final point of contact is achieved when the seeker becomes initiated into the "society" to which her teacher belongs. In this phase, the seeker becomes a messenger or teacher with a message somewhat different from that imparted to her. She is sharing in the teacher's consciousness but is not a carbon copy. In addition to that which has been given to her by her teacher, she is contributing something of her own. Her message now reflects her own awareness of the needs of humanity. This personal element is essential to enable one to focus a Universal consciousness sufficiently so that people in their ordinary lives can make contact with it.

The newness of the message is not due only to improvisation, it results from sharing her own personal being. To the extent that each personal life, each existence, brings with it its own set of experiences, it automatically has the potential to facilitate an understanding of human needs in some unique way. It is because of this unique understanding of needs that a new teacher can share her own being in some unique way and can bring a message that is old, yet new. She communicates a consciousness that she has received, yet one that has become entirely her own. The birth, mystical or otherwise, of a new messenger ends one phase of the endeavor of consciousness to grow and experience itself. At the same time, this event marks the beginning of another phase of expansion.

THE TEACHER AS LIVING SYMBOL AND INNER GUIDE

In his role as living symbol, the teacher also becomes a guide. It may be necessary for him to take his students to the very edge of despair so that their own inner guides can be activated, thus keeping them from falling into the abyss. In this function, the teacher is not someone who provides packaged answers, but is a living yardstick by which the student can measure himself. The teacher who stifles the development of this inner guide by attempting always to solve the problems of his students thinks he is doing them service. To the qualified and experienced teacher, the mind of his student is seen as a membrane separating the contents of concepts he has mastered from those over which the student has no mastery and may not even have knowledge. The teacher sees his mission as one of stretching this membrane to the point of translucency so that the light of understanding can come in to illuminate the unknown.

The first action of this light may be an uncovering of the poverty of the mind's possessions, resulting in a revelation which may challenge the seeker's ego or self-importance. In this exercise, both the seeker and the teacher must walk along a razor's edge, where, if the blind is leading the blind, they will "both fall into the ditch." This ditch can represent ill repute, difficulties with civil authorities, and so on. Many seekers have ended up in the psychiatric wards of hospitals due to the methods of various so-called teachers.

NATURAL LIMITATIONS OF THE TEACHER

In a certain respect, it is not possible for a teacher to communicate to a seeker what the seeker does not know already. Consequently, the knowledge that may flow from teacher to seeker cannot result in the experience of enlightenment by the seeker. When there appears to be a transfer of awareness from teacher to seeker, the teacher is in reality only a facilitator, a catalyst.

The teacher as facilitator brings about a recognition in the seeker by helping her reorganize the contents of her own psyche. The fact that the teacher cannot transfer enlightenment does not mean that there is no place for an interaction of the seeker of enlightenment and its possessor. However, the interaction can only become productive if the possessor of enlightenment is convinced of her inability to transfer it to anyone and the seeker is convinced that she is the only one that can help her own situation.

Even after the teacher has transferred knowledge, it will not do the seeker any good, because knowledge is lifeless. It is, in reality, only a waste product from inner psychological processing, and anyone who wants to collect knowledge is a collector of waste products. Just as a living organism takes in food, extracts what is valuable and discards the remainder, the seeker of Truth must take in aspiration and faith, distill the power-giving elements of under-standing, equilibrium, peace, and fairness, and let the rest go by.

When the teacher and the seeker get together, not only must the teacher not attempt to poison the seeker with the by-products of her personal understanding, she must provide the seeker with the means of obtaining spiritual food. She must teach the seeker courage. With courage, the seeker ceases to cling to the past and to fear the unknown. As a result, he finds aspiration and faith. This is the only valid reason for the seeker of enlightenment and its possessor to get together, so that the seeker is able to lose his appetite for the by-products of other people's understanding.

When the seeker sees how knowledge arises, he will be too busy getting rid of his own "waste products" to be bothered with that of others. He will also see that today's knowledge is the remains of yesterday's spiritual food. He will then cease to value knowledge for its own sake. When we are concerned with knowledge, we are preoccupied with cataloguing and accumulating. We attempt to isolate, to separate; to confer upon everything an existence independent of the totality of Consciousness and Life that constitute the Universe.

Notes, Chapter 9

1. I have very little confidence in the true transformative potential of channeled teachings by disembodied entities. For me, all the theories and philosophies delivered through channeling are really a sideshow. All true teachings with transformative power do more than provide ideas. They challenge us and mirror us to ourselves, revealing how we stand in each moment, how conscious or unconscious we are. Truly valuable teachings allow us to bring more of our essence into our waking moments.
2. An imposter is one who takes on the role of the teacher for its apparent benefits. He is essentially an unbeliever and knows he is an imposter. On the other hand, the charlatan is sincere and a believer, but does not understand the full range of responsibilities that being a teacher demands. Where the imposter is driven by contempt for the spiritual, the charlatan is driven by ego needs.

IO   False Dawn or Early Sunrise? Distinguishing Spiritual from Psychic Experiences

In the West Indies where I grew up, I was exposed to a phenomenon that I have often reflected upon on account of its similarity with a particular aspect of the spiritual quest. It has to do with the cues that some rural folks rely on to alert them to the onset of daybreak. There were many poor people in my village who did not own an alarm clock, and consequently had to rely on the crowing of the neighborhood roosters to wake them up. On particularly bright moonlit nights (during the waning phases of the full moon), the roosters become confused and begin crowing to signal daybreak much before its time. When this occurs, the people who depend on them awake to what they anticipate to be the approaching dawn. As they have no way of alerting themselves to the roosters' mistake, they set out on their journeys for their daily chores on their farm plots, which were at times several miles' distance from their homes. Sometimes they do not complete their journeys on account of being engulfed in darkness as the moon falls below the horizon or becomes obscured by dark clouds. It is then too late to turn back to their homes, but at the same time, not light enough for them to do their work. They then have to bide their time and wait for the real daybreak.

There is similarity here with the way some spiritual seekers relate to experience they feel to be of a spiritual nature and for which they may not have the proper frame of reference. The problem is compounded nowadays as many individuals engage in psychospiritual and other techniques such as meditation, fasting, yoga postures, and breathing exercises that, at earlier times, were restricted to the protected environments of monasteries and ashrams. The result is that they are having various kinds of spiritual and psychic experiences for which they might not have the proper preparation. Worse still, some may take up these practices with the sole objective of having these experiences. They might have read of them in the many available books that deal with the transformational process in its various manifestations.

There is a misconception on many fronts that the development of psychic abilities is the objective of spiritual work. Consequently, a real need exists for people concerned with transformation to gain a perspective on the place of spiritual and psychic experiences in the transformational process. The New Age press and notice boards are full of advertisements offering classes on reading auras, healing, dowsing, trance mediumship, and so forth. No wonder so many people feel that spiritual work is synonymous with the development of these hidden "talents" and "powers." Over the years, when people I know became aware of my involvement in transformational pursuits, many frequently asked, "Do you see auras? Do you read minds? Do you have visions?"

While the motivation behind these questions may have been innocent enough, they still betrayed a lack of understanding of the differences between spiritual and psychic experiences and the proper role of a truly spiritual experience in one's spiritual work. To arrive at this understanding we need, first, to distinguish between genuine spiritual experiences and those normally recognized as psychic.

SPIRITUAL AND PSYCHIC EXPERIENCES CONTRASTED

A spiritual experience may take many manifestations — a dream, a vision, a "visitation," an impression, or a personal "miracle." The form is not what is of importance, it is the effect that it has on one's being that is. *An experience is spiritual by virtue of its potential to enhance our perception of the world, or to completely transform our life.* A psychic experience, on the other hand, may be recurring, sporadic, or sustained. It may expand an individual's normal powers of observation, in the case of clairvoyance, or increase his or her powers of command over the physical environment, such as psychokinesis. In addition, there may be many other experiences such as out-of-body phenomena and UFO sightings, which fall into a category all their own.

Whereas spiritual experiences are the result of spiritual development, and consequently have a wholesome effect on one's life, most psychic experiences are the result of a personality imbalance. This will become evident to anyone who has had the opportunity to closely observe someone who professes such powers and gives a lot of attention to them, whether to exercise them or to develop them further. It is then that the "cracks" in the being and the "hemorrhaging" they lead to become noticeable. This hemorrhaging is in the form of a diminishing of the will, emotional instability, poor physical health, and a loss of intellectual ability. This is quite similar to what happens when a bicycle tube becomes weak in one spot and "balloons out" and may eventually burst. In saying this, I am aware that this does not fit everyone who wants to be known as a "psychic," but it covers the majority of psychics I have personally known. The only general exception that one can make to this observation is when those who give vent to such "abilities" do so in the disciplined framework of a program of genuine spiritual development. In such a situation, the psychic does not actively pursue information through psychic means.

Another way in which psychic and spiritual experiences differ is in their effect on the general human community. Whereas a spiritual experience induces one into a more cooperative arrangement with the human community, a psychic experience or a faculty can reinforce the tendency towards separativeness in the individual so endowed. Let us look at the example of seeing auras to show how this works.

There are a great number of books available on the human aura and its interpretation. Usually, the gist of this interpretation is the reading of an individual's character. People who think of the ability to read auras as a gift might think of this as adding to their ability to discern individuals who are of noble character from the ignoble (honest from dishonest individuals). This would supposedly make it easier for them as they choose their business associates, friends, mates, and the like. Here, I must confess, at an earlier stage of my own spiritual work I thought wistfully how much easier life would have been for me had I this "ability" to sort out the good from the bad.

Spiritual work is, however, not that simple; neither should it be. Collectively, we have become much too cautious. We are too preoccupied with concerns as to which person will or will not defraud or take advantage of us. The more spiritual we become, the less we find it necessary to protect ourselves from those of unsavory character. Just as we use one hand to wash the other without being afraid that the soiled hand will dirty the clean, the transformational process in its collective scope is facilitated when good and bad interact. The spiritually developed must become catalysts to help those of lesser understanding evolve. Actually, the extent to which we separate people into good and bad categories is an indication of our need for further spiritual development.

When we are sufficiently developed, we know how to look and find all people good, as Laotzu reminds us: "I find good people good and I find bad people good, if I am good enough."[1] It is not that morality is not important; but if we have sufficient understanding, we would see that although individuals may act inappropriately in many of the situations of life, most only want the best for themselves. It is in seeing this good that people want for themselves that enables us to find bad people good. The ability to see this good in another is the only psychic ability that must be desired.

INTERPRETING SPIRITUAL EXPERIENCES

An important characteristic of spiritual experiences is that they manifest themselves to individuals in terms relative to their level of understanding and development. The individual modes through which we encounter the Universe vary because we live in a symbolic Universe. The main implication of living in a symbolic Universe is that Reality as it is perceived and encountered is not exactly the same for everyone. Our individual means of perception convey different meanings to each of us. Because of this, if different individuals need to receive the same meaning, in terms of emotional intensity (so that a particular aspect of spiritual growth can commence), different means must be utilized to convey this. In general, the more aware we are that Reality, as we experience it, is symbolic, the less we will have need to be communicated to in symbolic terms. The less aware we are of the symbolic nature of our Universe, the more necessary it is for Life to communicate to us in symbolic terms.

A spiritual experience is symbolic and does not have meaning in and of itself. Its significance is relative to where we have been, where we are headed, and where we are at present. Behind every experience is a principle that wants us to make its acquaintance. The mode chosen to get us to look in its direction depends on how sensitive we are.

We can draw an analogy between the ways in which events intercede between us and a principle and the various modalities that we can use to get in touch with one another. If we want to get in touch with someone as quickly as possible, we would usually resort to the telephone, provided that the other person has one. If he has no telephone, we would use the mail, provided that he has a fixed address. If he has no fixed address, we have to get a message to him through someone else who sees him more frequently than we do. Failing all these, we have to wait for a chance encounter with this individual. Similarly, the spiritual principles that want us to acquaint ourselves with them would have to use whatever means we make available to them to contact us.

The mode chosen by a principle to get us to look in its direction always depends on how receptive we are. The most direct way that we can make the acquaintance of a principle is through the faculty of intuition. With intuition, every experience has the potential to be a spiritual experience, because every experience has the potential to take us to a clearer understanding of the purpose of our life.

THE RELATIVITY OF SPIRITUAL EXPERIENCES

By generalizing a bit more, we can classify the channels that spiritual lessons we need can take before we become aware of them. We can classify such channels into four categories, from least to most symbolic. In each case, it is the degree of symbolism utilized that is the determining factor. By symbolism in this specific context, we mean "conformity with everyday experiences." Thus, the more elements of our everyday, material reality that contribute to an event, the more symbolic it is.

The first channel of contact is facilitated through our "direct understanding" of principles; the second, through charged emotions evoked through religious images; the third, through enticements that utilize the desire nature; and fourth, through negative reinforcement, such as fear.

With the first channel of contact we can become directly acquainted with a spiritual principle in meditation, contemplation, and spiritual exercises such as prayer and fasting. Through these heightened states of being, contact is made with spiritual principles on the mental plane. Provided that we have developed the habit of giving expression to principles as we understand them, we receive new inputs by way of direct knowing, through intuition. This faculty, intuition, comes into full-blown operation when we have exhausted our capacity for reason. A good operational definition of intuition is *the functioning of the whole being, operating as one unit, without stress.*

With the second channel of contact, our emotions provide the mode of transmission. We may be contacted through a dream, vision, or other form of communication, such as hearing a voice. Usually the object of the dream or vision may be a religious figure of primary importance to us. A Christian might have an encounter with Jesus or, in the case of a Catholic, with the Holy Virgin Mary, and so forth. Such a mode of contact works because it causes us to make a fuller commitment to beliefs that we already hold, but that we may not have actively practiced.

With the third channel, our desire nature is utilized. We may be enticed to act out of the desire for personal benefit. Some aspects of the Scriptures fulfill this role, since they usually promise heavenly rewards if certain precepts are followed. The medium of dreams and visions may also be utilized here, but in this case the symbols encountered may be less emotionally charged.

Finally, the last channel utilized is one of last resort, such as fear. Near-death experiences have been known to change many a person for the better. However, the means of communicating spiritual principles at this level may be less drastic, such as ordinary hardships and difficulties we may experience in life. We might have to "touch bottom" before we realize the need to change and adopt new and nobler pursuits.

Although some of the experiences that compose the fourth channel of contact may be ordinary, they are nevertheless symbolic in that their function is to serve some higher purpose. This may explain, in part, some aspects of suffering that "good" people sometimes go through. According to the writer of the biblical book of Ecclesiastes, "There is a just man that perisheth in his righteousness, and there is a wicked man that prolongeth his life in his wickedness" (Eccles. 7:15). The point he is making is that the physical conditions of our life are not always a sign of Divine merit or demerit. What is important is the spiritual insight we are able to extract form every situation, be it "good" or "bad."

Since spiritual experiences, in real life, may not always arrange themselves in the clear-cut categories we've just described, but may come as a mixture of several, it may be necessary for us to decipher our experiences to understand how certain bits of information are to be digested. This is of particular importance at the second (emotional) and third (desire nature) channels of communication. At these levels, we must first discover the levels at which the symbolic content of experiences must be interpreted, whether we should relate to them at a personal or an impersonal level. To assist in this task, C. G. Jung's approach of classifying symbols into those that have content of a personal nature and those that have content of a collective nature will prove useful. The following example will relate how helpful this procedure might be.

Some years ago, I was contacted by an individual who was seeking to start a series of spiritual communities, actually, seven in number; six of them were to be based on land and the seventh based on an ocean-going schooner, which was also to serve as a means of communicating between the six. The individual was basing the justification for this project on a dream-vision she had in which she clearly saw six land-based cities and an ocean-going schooner serving as a floating city and forming a connection between the land-based ones. At the time I was contacted she was still working on the concept of this chain of communities and was hoping to interest enough people to begin a funding drive.

Now this dream had a great deal of emotional content for this individual and there appeared to be no doubt in her mind that something of significance was communicated to her. However, she accepted what she saw at face value and did not seek an explanation to it at any level but the literal, physical one. If she had sought an explanation at another level, she might have realized that what she saw made more sense when interpreted at a symbolic level. In the first case, the symbolic significance of the number seven should have suggested to her that the communication she received might not have involved a collective revelation, but a personal one using symbols from the Universal "treasure house," or from the Collective Unconscious, in the sense that Jung used the term. As such, she might have discovered that the dream contained personal insights using symbolism that relates to the chakra system according to the formulations of kundalini yoga. Perhaps, this dream-vision should have been accepted as a hint concerning her potential for awakening her own psychic energy and the energization of her chakras. The seven cities in this sense would have related to her seven chakras rather than to seven literal cities.

Even if this person in question did not have a familiarity with the chakra system, she should have known that the interpretation of her dream was to be found at other than the physical level. For example, what was to be the significance in founding seven cities? As spiritual communities go, one should be enough, if a practical interpretation was to be given to her dream. Any Universal principle that can be represented by seven cities can also be adequately and fully represented by one.

The misinterpretation of an experience does not always leave the experiencer with nothing more severe than a broken dream or a stalled endeavor. A more serious consequence can be ego inflation, with tragic consequences for oneself and others. We shall next consider this grave danger of misinterpreting and misunderstanding psychic experiences.

DANGERS FROM MISINTERPRETING EXPERIENCES

In his biography of C. G. Jung, Laurens van der Post[2] writes about an individual in history who had a profound spiritual experience as a young man. He subsequently took this as an indication that he was chosen by Providence for some special destiny.

This experience took place in a trench during World War I. While asleep in a trench with his comrades, this individual had a very disturbing dream from which he awoke in a cold sweat. In the dream he had the overwhelming premonition that he was about to be engulfed in a torrent of earth and mud. Still in a daze, he ran outside, away from the protection of the trench. As soon as he was out, he looked in disbelief as a mortar shell exploded into the trench and killed all of his comrades. This individual began to take this incident as a sign that he was selected by Fate for a special destiny. In some respects, he was, but what a destiny! That individual was Adolf Hitler.

The immediate danger of any experience that can be classified as spiritual is that it could lead to ego inflation. When this occurs, it is impossible to get the lesson that an experience is trying to teach. In his analysis of the Hitler experience, Jung said that Hitler should have taken it as a warning. The torrent of earth and mud that scared him out of his slumber was psychic mud that would later find expression through him with his all-too-willing consent. The dream was to be taken as a warning and a message that it was possible to escape this fate. The message was, however, lost as the recipient of the experience felt that he was being favored. He felt that he was "somebody special." This is how one falls victim to ego inflation.

There are a few cardinal rules to be followed to ensure that a spiritual experience does not lead to ego inflation and eventual ruin. First, when having an experience that might be regarded as spiritual, we must not be hasty in claiming a revelation or Divine visitation. We must wait for the other shoe to drop, in a manner of speaking. If we are to be the recipient of an important truth, or a new religion, or some earth-shattering revelation, the message would be repeated. One never volunteers for such a task. One is always conscripted, sometimes kicking and screaming in protest.

Even if we are genuinely to be the recipient of something significant, it is possible that the message might not be imparted all at once. If we are hasty and pitch tent or hang up a professional shingle, we might be doing so on only part of the message.

The other principle we need to observe is that we must determine how our experience corresponds with the experiences and revelations of others. We also need to determine what implications we can derive at a collective level from our experience or revelation. For example, does our revelation form a continuing pattern of unfolding with the revelations of others? Does it have the potential to further the growth and improvement of human society if it is adopted?

When these quality checks are ignored and we hastily pitch tent and hang up shingle, the structures we've built on our revelation may falter. When this occurs we might experience a feeling of rejection and may succumb to a spiritual paranoia. We might then feel that God has given us a mission and has forsaken us. This creates a most destructive situation because we might feel resentful towards God, feeling that God has betrayed us. At this point the problem gets worse. Where does one go when he feels betrayed by God? With such negative emotions seething within, a person becomes open and receptive to tremendous negative energies. There are all sorts of negative psychic forces that would love to find someone in such a resentful situation, because they can team up with that person. The consequence is that the individual might feel really powerful for a time, but eventually destroy himself and take others with him.

I believe that this is where many spiritual visionaries and charismatic leaders of various movements go wrong, sometimes with tragic consequences, like the Jim Jones fiasco. How can we tell when an individual who claims to be a teacher and leader is falling apart? This question is particularly relevant for one who may be thinking of following a teacher.

The first thing to be aware of is that the process of development is not an even one throughout an individual's lifetime. At the outset, one may be the recipient of a very clear vision, a very strong mandate. Over time, the strength of that mandate may weaken as the clarity of that vision begins to fade. If one has allowed the original vision to inflate her ego, she begins to feel desperate. She may feel that it is up to her to keep up appearances, so she begins to dig deep and in the process, begins to dredge up material from her own subconscious.

Since the subconscious is a hotbed of complexes and unassimilated experiences, the individual will have to deal with all sorts of "tests and trials." This is the point at which she may feel that God has abandoned her. She may feel that she is a lamb that has been deliberately thrown to the wolves. Actually, the one who has succeeded in getting this far spiritually must begin to take responsibility for whatever work of a spiritual nature she has started. She must carry a burden for humanity. It is not enough that she regards herself as one chosen for a special mission. In order to keep on track with the way in which her vision should unfold, she must distribute or "subcontract" some of the responsibility for that original vision to people around her, to share that vision with others. Ego inflation keeps one from sharing, and consequently one burns out.

There is an additional factor at work when we try to give embodiment to a vision. It is that spiritual unfolding must express itself in the general context of human development and evolution. The recipient of a vision must create a point of contact with humanity where that vision can be translated into concepts and terms of reference relevant to the ordinary individual. The first task in establishing such a contact is to share that vision with others and not use it to demand special status and unquestioned obedience.

DEVELOPING THE INTUITION

Earlier, we defined intuition as the result of the whole being functioning as one unit without stress. As a faculty, intuition is the ability to see through the veil of the symbolic into the Real. It is the ability to detect equivalence, to see higher principles in action in the ordinary world.

The difference between intuition and psychic phenomena is quite marked. To illustrate this difference, we'll resort to the following analogy. Let us assume we are following the course of a river from its source to the sea. If we are at a very high elevation and very short distance from the sea, we will expect to encounter many discontinuities in the course of the river. We might find rapids or a waterfall, or both. On the other hand, if we are far from the sea and not too far up in elevation, the course of the river would be more even, without discontinuities. We might even find a lake along its course.

The first case — where there are rapids and waterfalls in the river — aptly represents the functioning of psychic powers. It represents a discontinuity between the outer world of form and the inner world of principles. The second case — where there is a smooth flow to the sea — represents the functioning of intuition. In this analogy, the main difference between the ways in which psychic powers and intuition function lies in the extent of intermediation between the inner and outer levels of consciousness. This intermediation is in the form of understanding the relationship between form and substance, principle and manifestation. It is really the ability to see interrelationships, to see larger wholes and to function on the basis of being part of these larger wholes.

At the mental level, we have to learn to think in the language of symbolism instead of thinking in the vernacular of everyday language. This facility is developed when we begin to cultivate the investigative and nurturing aspects of the mind as opposed to its more judgmental one. Rather than judging and criticizing, we must learn to ask questions and make comments that are conducive to the solicitation of more information. Too often, we accept the written and spoken word as the final reality of another person's state of being, even when we know fully that our own words, oral and written, never exhaust the contents of our own minds. The investigative and witnessing aspects of the mind take us beyond words to the states of being from which those words take form.

Notes, Chapter 10

1. Witter Bynner (translator), *The Way of Life According to Laotzu* (New York: Capricorn Books, 1962), 56.
2. Laurens van der Post, *Jung and the Story of Our Time* (New York: Pantheon Books, 1975), 19–20.

I I   The Adoption of the Body

THE PLACE OF THE BODY IN TRANSFORMATION

Traditionally, our notions about spirituality do not figure in how the body can share in spiritual awakening. The outstanding exception is the work of Sri Aurobindo and his associate and beneficiary of his mantle, known as *Mother*.[1] For Sri Aurobindo and Mother, humanity is standing at the threshold of a new spiritual realization that will have impact on all aspects of the human being and our way of life on the earth. They envisioned our collective transformation taking a quantum leap to a new level of reality that is more inclusive. They saw the physical body serving as the bridge to this new consciousness.

Ideas similar to Sri Aurobindo's and Mother's were held by Teilhard de Chardin, a Jesuit priest and scientist and contemporary of Sri Aurobindo. Similar ideas were expressed by the apostle Paul, almost two thousand years previously. Teilhard de Chardin[2] saw all of creation coming to a spiritual realization, which he termed the *Omega Point*. As for St. Paul, he called this transition the *Resurrection* — which will result in the "adoption" of the physical body by the Divine Spirit. The name Sri Aurobindo gave to his vision of human spiritual realization is the *Supramental Manifestation*.

As we have already observed in Chapter 3, Sri Aurobindo's context for the transformation of humanity views the present human being as transitional, a temporary phenomenon that would be superseded. The key to this succession lies in rescuing the body from the tyranny of the mind, thus transforming it to the clarity and levity of which it is capable. Sri Aurobindo and Mother made the body the focus of their spiritual teaching and practice. Their goal was to bring the Light of spiritual aspiration and Realization down into the very cells of the body and thus start a "contagion" that would spread and affect all of humanity.

Not too long ago, this view as to how transformation achieved by the few can be shared by the many would have been regarded as purely mystical — without a scientific basis. Now, the scientific evidence is available to assure us that not only is it possible, but necessary as a mechanism for the sharing of evolutionary progress among the members of a species. Just about the time when I became captivated by the Aurobindo vision, I discovered in a book some information that supplied the scientific evidence to convince me that this vision foretells our collective destiny.

The author of that book wrote about how a potato-washing habit became transmitted throughout a colony of monkeys on Koshima Island, off the coast of Japan, and then to other colonies on separate islands, even though there were no physical means of interaction between the different colonies. As the story goes, this potato-washing practice was first invented by a juvenile monkey, who taught it to her mother, who then taught it to her mate. Other monkeys copied the practice until it was adopted throughout the colony as an accepted practice. Eventually, monkeys on other islands were observed to be doing the same thing. This phenomenon has since become one of the popular new paradigms of the transformational movement. It has even been used as the seed idea for a book, *The Hundredth Monkey*, by Ken Keyes, Jr.[3]

This story of the Koshima Island monkeys, together with the Aurobindo vision, spoke so clearly to my heart that, for a while, I used it as an illustration whenever I had occasion to explain to friends the significance of the work of Sri Aurobindo, Mother, and many others concerned with transformation. An incident took place on one such occasion that is worth recounting. I was a dinner guest one Sunday afternoon at the home of a spiritual teacher from India and his disciples, and brought up this story to illustrate my personal approach to the transformational quest. As soon as I finished telling the story of the monkeys, someone turned on the television set. The program, "Wild Kingdom," with its host, Merlon Perkins, came on. The subject of his program was the same monkeys of Koshima Island and the phenomenon of how their potato-washing habit got spread among different island colonies without the benefit of physical contact. That, of course, caused a stir in the little group.

The string of coincidences that so neatly orchestrated the events of my discussion of this phenomenon and the television program were simply remarkable. I had never seen this episode of "Wild Kingdom," and did not know it existed. For my comments and its broadcast to be so closely juxtaposed was quite synchronistic. Someone had to turn on the television set at that precise time and select that specific channel from the more than thirty available. At that time, I took the incident as an endorsement of the validity of the point I was making. It came as a Cosmic Amen, if you will.

FORETASTES OF GLORY?

It is possible that the transformational "contagion" that Sri Aurobindo and Mother sought has already begun. Over the past couple of decades we have witnessed a tremendous explosion of interest in the body and its secrets. People are concerning themselves with physical activity and fitness as never before. While each individual who feels so motivated has his or her own specific reasons for participating in these activities, each one is nevertheless responding to the aspiration of the body to attain its own perfection. It is as if the body is no longer satisfied with the crumbs of attention that grudgingly fall from the table of its tyrannical master, the mind.

As individuals begin to attune to the body, systems within it that have heretofore remained dormant will awaken, and we will witness the progressive resurrection of the body. The "prodigal son" will indeed return to his place of honor in the trinity of body, mind, and spirit.

There are several bodily experiences I have had which have served to reinforce my belief in the importance of the body to transformation. I will now relate some of these.

One early November evening, I set out from Toronto with a friend to attend a weekend yoga retreat in a small town north of Toronto. Normally, this would be a one-hour drive, but on this particular evening it had begun to snow as darkness set in, making driving treacherous and slow. To complicate matters, the directions given us to the place where the retreat was to be held were quite imprecise. What was supposed to be a two-mile stretch on the directional map turned out to be more like five, and so on.

As our journey progressed, the weather and visibility worsened, and driving became progressively more hazardous. After about two hours of driving, we got close to our destination, which was at the bottom of an incline. At this point, the road took a very steep grade and several sharp turns. We were quite unprepared for this steep incline as we rounded one of these turns. The car picked up speed and my first impulse was to slow down. Since the road was covered with snow I was afraid to brake so I shifted into a lower gear. At that point, the car went out of control and spun around at least 360 degrees. After what seemed to be an endless moment, it came to rest with the rear wheels perched precipitously on the edge of a roadside ditch, which was perhaps about five feet deep and about as wide.

As if to express our relief and gratitude at being saved by what amounted to us to be something no less than a miracle, my friend and I embraced and uttered prayers of thanksgiving. The real miracle for me, though, was what transpired in that moment of absolute helplessness as the car spun out of control. At that moment, something in me seemed to have disengaged, snapped. It was as if I was just watching the action from somewhere else. At no time at all did I experience fear or anxiety. After the car came to a stop, a sensation similar to numbness, or emptiness, remained. The only sensation of myself I had was a throb emanating from my heart area. This was not an unusual sensation for me but it was the first time I had experienced it outside of sitting meditation. At a particular stage of my meditation exercise I would shift to level after level of awareness until I arrive at a state where feelings and thoughts disappear and I would become just a pulsating mass of energy. On this occasion, I went directly to this stage from one of normal waking consciousness.

We arrived at our destination without further incident, and as the evening progressed I became more and more devoid of personal sensations and thoughts. As the retreat was convened, we met in the rented hall for introductions, then in accordance with the program paired off with others to share the results of different psychological exercises we engaged in. We had to spend a few minutes with one person, then change to someone else.

Some of the people I paired with sensed the energy that had enveloped me but could not understand what was going on or identify its source. One individual, as he talked with me, broke off the conversation and confessed that he could not think straight as his mind was "turning on and off." He seemed to enjoy this sensation, which was new to him. I knew that what he was sensing was connected to the pulsations that I, or rather my body, was emanating. However, I did not say anything about the source of his mind turning on and off. Another individual, the friend who rode up with me (and who was somewhat clairvoyant), said that she sensed a pulsation impacting her and when she looked around the room, was able to correlate this with a brilliant light that flashed intermittently with the pulsation. She said that this was coming from me. I had not revealed to her anything of what had happened to me, nor what the experience of the other individual was. My "normal" self did not return again until the following day.

There have been many other experiences involving the body. On almost all of these occasions, some sort of physical activity was involved. On several of them, I was engaged in a game of tennis or squash when a shift in consciousness occurred. Every action thereafter was as if it was directed from somewhere other than my normal, historical self. In the early years after the initial awakening experiences, I found it very difficult to keep my attention on my tennis game or get myself psyched up enough to play to win. I had a resistance deep within me that kept me from giving my all in competitive events (and still do, to some degree). However, on these occasions, every action would be perfectly executed, particularly my service. People I previously played tennis with would approach in wonderment and ask if I had been taking lessons. After one such performance, my partner enquired if I had been doing TM since the last time we played.

The first couple of times I played under these conditions I was under the illusion that this newly acquired prowess would last forever. I even fantasized that with this incredible energy at my disposal I could still become a professional even at my late stage of life (i.e., after thirty). Imagine my disappointment at finding that it was not there the next time I went to play. I was my usual clumsy self!

Another experience with this energy took place one early morning in the picture-postcard setting of a recreational lake community around the Georgian Bay area of Ontario, where I was participating in a yoga retreat. I had gone for an early morning walk with several fellow retreaters. I was dressed in warm, heavy clothes and was wearing a pair of heavy hiking boots. On the way back to the campground, about a mile and a bit out, someone suggested we run back. I am no jogger or runner and showed this ignorance by starting out at a pace far too rapid for my stamina. Some of my companions shouted at me to slow down, telling me that I was starting out too fast and, with some amusement, warned that they'd soon catch up to me and pass me when I gave out. I quite expected them to be right about this, as my purpose in rushing on ahead was to see how far I could go. I had every intention to quit when I reached my breaking point.

As that point came, I found my legs turning into wet sponge, too flaccid to lift my heavy hiking boots. I was ready to collapse. Instead of giving up, I spoke audibly to my legs, saying "Come on legs, don't give up on me now." At that very moment, a surge of energy came into my legs and my lungs, and practically motorized my legs. I was able to continue running at the fast pace at which I had begun and arrived at the campground far ahead of the rest. Naturally, everyone thought that I was an accomplished runner. But how does one begin to explain to someone who has not experienced the magic of the body's hidden energies? What fascinated me most about this incident is that the body responded independently to the urging of my voice. Also, what I experienced cannot be categorized as a second wind since I have also experienced the latter. They belong to two totally different mechanisms.

Another experience quite similar took place during a run I had on a beach in Goa, India. I had taken a walk — about four miles or so from the beach hotel where I was staying. After my walk in one direction, I gave in to an impulse to run back at least part of the way to the hotel. Everything was so idyllic — early morning sun, beautiful beach, exhilarating, fresh, salty air, and the sound of the waves beating on the shore. During my run back, I almost gave up several times because of physical exhaustion, but I carried on. At about the two-mile mark, I felt absolutely that I was going to drop, but I kept on. What happened was similar to what I experienced a year and a half previously at Georgian Bay. This time was different as the energization of my body was more diffused — the entire body was in ecstasy. When I finished the run, the feeling of bliss in every cell of my body continued for several hours. I often wished that there was some predictable way to tap into this wonderful, incredible energy. Imagine the work one could accomplish under such conditions!

WORKING CONSCIOUSLY WITH THE BODY

There has been an explosion of therapies in recent years based on the discovery of the body's ability to release stored psychological hurts and traumas. We have had bioenergetics, rebirthing, and various forms of deep tissue massage. And we have had Hatha Yoga, tai chi, and other martial art disciplines for thousands of years, although they have only recently been imported to the West. These body-centered therapies suggest to me that, in addition to our becoming more aware of the role of the body, the body itself is also becoming more yielding, more responsive, making it even more imperative that we find ways to solicit the cooperation of the body in our transformational work.

Having at one time done Hatha Yoga rather intensively for a period of just over a year, I can vouch for the efficacy of that discipline in bringing one into a greater state of receptivity to higher energies. I discontinued my Hatha Yoga practice because it interfered with my capacity for ordinary work. It would reinforce certain meditative and ecstatic states that made it difficult for me to concentrate on certain tasks. To be fair to Hatha Yoga itself, many of its practitioners do not have this problem. Perhaps my experience is an isolated case, precipitated by my own spontaneous awakening experiences, which occurred before I ever took part in yogic exercises.

The body's sensitivity can be augmented, allowing it to participate even more in the transformational quest, as I discovered some years ago when, without the aid of ideology, I adopted a vegetarian diet. This step was taken quite spontaneously; the eating of meat came to seem quite unnatural to me. Also, at this time it was only with great discomfort that I was able to pass by the meat counter at the supermarket. It is hard to tell which came first, the sensitivity or the change in diet. Whatever the cause and effect relationship, there is no doubt in my mind that this turn of events was a necessary step for me, as I try to have a deeper sense of relationship to the world within and about me.

Notes, Chapter 11

1. Hereafter referred to as Mother.
2. Pierre Teilhard de Chardin, *The Phenomenon of Man* (London: Fontana Books, 1965).
3. Ken Keyes, Jr., *The Hundredth Monkey* (Coos Bay, Or.: Vision Books, 1982).

12 The Enigma of Spiritual Realization

CULMINATION OF THE TRANSFORMATIONAL IMPULSE

Just as the reproduction cycle culminates in labor and delivery, so the transformational impulse culminates in various degrees of spiritual Realization. Consequently, the question most spiritual seekers are interested in is whether there is a direct correspondence between a person's inner realization of Truth and his outer life condition. In this specific context, spiritual realization is tricky to assess, as the quotation we have previously cited from the book of Ecclesiastes testifies: "There is a just man that perisheth in his righteousness, and there is a wicked man that prolongeth his life in his wickedness."

The issue of spiritual realization is one that has plagued seekers of every age. To help us get a handle on it, let us return to the "Sun Woman" of Revelation whom we visited rather briefly in the first chapter. At the point where we left her she was just about to give birth. Before we can get any insight here that might be helpful, we have to examine what the Sun Woman represents. We will recall that she was clothed with the Sun, had the Moon beneath her feet, and a crown of twelve stars on her head.

To me, the Sun Woman represents each and every one of us as we are engaged in the work of distilling meaning from life. She represents the focal point of different realities: the Sun, representing life, love, and wisdom; the Moon, representing the emotions; and the crown of stars, representing the maturing effect of time on the mental faculties. The Child to which she is about to give birth represents the synthesis of the different realities of life, love, and wisdom. In the context of earthly life, the Child represents spiritual realization.

The author of Revelation points out that while the Sun Woman was waiting to give birth, there was also another event waiting to be manifest: a "great red dragon" was waiting to devour the Child as soon as it was born. This great red dragon is the ego, and, in relation to our personal efforts at the transformation of consciousness, it wants to realize and immediately consume whatever proceeds of striving may result from our efforts. In other words, patience is not a characteristic of the ego-centered consciousness.

In order to protect the Child from the dragon, it was caught up to God as soon as it was born. This mythological drama surrounding the Sun Woman is pointing out that, from the perspective of earthly life, most of our efforts expended to acquire spiritual consciousness may at first appear to have no effect. This is because the results of our efforts build up below the threshold of our awareness. In our transformational work, we may work very hard to refine our consciousness yet feel that little progress has been made in bringing about any substantive change in our material reality.

I recall a conversation I had some years ago with an individual who was having difficulty securing the type of employment situation that she thought she deserved. She said to me, "I feel that I've achieved a certain realization and don't think I should be experiencing so much difficulty getting a job that is suitable." To my understanding, this is exactly the sort of thing that we are protected from when the Child is "caught up to God and to His throne."

If it were entirely up to us to choose the point of realization of our spiritual striving, we would find it very difficult, if not impossible, to do so with the required discernment. There are two reasons for this. First, we might be too hasty to lay claim to a realization and shortchange ourselves in the process. Second, we might not be able to recognize that for which we are seeking even when it presents itself to us. These two problems define what we may call the two horns of the realization dilemma. There are two illustrations in the Bible that demonstrate these problems rather well, and we shall study them a bit closely to gain some relevant insight.

THE FIRST HORN OF THE REALIZATION DILEMMA

The first horn of the realization dilemma, choosing the appropriate point of realization for the proceeds of our spiritual efforts, is illustrated in Genesis the story of Jacob and Esau. Esau, the older son of Isaac, in a moment of desperation signed over his birthright to his brother Jacob for a bowl of red lentil soup.[1] Later on he felt a great deal of remorse but could do nothing about it. Too late, he realized that he had exchanged a more meaningful, but more distant realization for one that was immediate, but not so meaningful.

The problem that Esau encountered is not that uncommon among spiritual seekers today. It is one of the hardest things to come to terms with the apparent contradiction of being committed to the spiritual life only to have the affairs of one's outer life begin falling into disarray. We are tempted to settle for a way of life that is, perhaps, not so idealistic, that is more pragmatic and "sensible." Sometimes, this decision is made because we feel that there should be harmony in our outer life commensurate with harmony in the inner one. Usually we take disorganization and chaos in the outer life as a sign that something is spiritually amiss. What we have to realize here is that there is absolutely no *a priori* reason why the outer life should correspond to inner harmony in this particular spiritual dispensation. We should therefore regard this notion, calling for congruity between the inner and outer life, as The Great Lie.[2]

The lack of correspondence between one's spiritual level of being and one's outer level circumstances exists for a particular reason. This is to impress upon us that we are not so much aiming for an individual or personal spiritual realization as for a Collective Realization. The fact that we may feel defeat at every turn, or feel that all our efforts are to no avail, does not mean that we are not accomplishing something significant for the collective aspect of the transformation. The struggles we face are there to spur us on. They get us to intensify our aspirations at the very point where we would have slowed down to rest on our laurels and enjoy the proceeds of our work. This intensification of aspirations also has the effect of attenuating the ego.[3]

Another point we often forget is that the transformation of our consciousness is a joint endeavor between us and a level of reality that is already perfected. The symbolism of the Sun Woman also hints at this. Recall that she was blending a human reality (in the form of the Moon at her feet) and a heavenly one (the Sun). The Sun, representing life, love, and light, is a contribution from Above in a joint endeavor. Thus, as the "senior partner" in this joint venture, the Higher Reality, whom we might call God, sees to it that the proceeds are protected pending the full completion of the process of transformation at the collective level, or until there is no longer any ego-directed interest in the outcome of the process.

Those of us who are satisfied with a more immediate realization would be giving validity and reinforcement to our present false "reality." A case in point is someone who loses faith in the appropriateness and validity of her spiritual pursuits on their own ground and looks to the world for such validation. Here she might fall into the trap of regarding success in the form of fame and riches as a sign that her spiritual pursuits meet with Divine approval. When we are able to consummate the quest in material glory, no room is left for Sacred Space in the heart. It is this room that provides the womb for the new to incubate and grow.

While we are on the subject of Sacred Space, we can find a very good demonstration in the way that some businesses leave themselves open to technological innovations by designing equipment with features that make them adaptable to future applications. I recall some years ago the telephone company introduced a new telephone with an extra button with an asterisk on it. The button had no immediate function, and the explanation given by the telephone company for its presence was that it was reserved for future use. This is essentially what the Sacred Space idea is about — something reserved for future use.

There is another problem that comes to mind when we try to unravel the enigma of spiritual realization, this time, that of suffering. There are many variations in our attitudes and explanations to suffering. There are even some of us who see suffering as something outside of God's Will and Plan.

THE SECOND HORN OF THE REALIZATION DILEMMA

In the twenty-second chapter of the gospel of Matthew there is a story about a wedding celebration and the ejection of one guest who did not have a wedding garment. It says there that a nobleman gave a wedding feast for his son and invited the important people to attend. They refused, each one offering the perfect excuse as to why he or she could not attend. Upon receiving their rebuff, the nobleman was furious, but decided that the wedding feast must go on nevertheless. He sent servants into the neighborhood and bade them to grab hold of whomever they could find and compel them to attend. They were to go along the main street and the side roads. While the celebration was in progress, the nobleman approached one of the guests and inquired as to why he was not wearing a wedding garment. This confrontation occurred despite the fact that the nobleman himself had established an open-door policy. In present day customs, the guest's predicament would be equivalent to not having a tuxedo at a function where one is required. But what are the chances, if from the main street and side roads of a town we invited everyone we could find to a wedding celebration, that all of them will conform to the required dress code? Rather slim, to say the least.

At a literal level, we might feel that this was unfair of the nobleman to expect everyone to adhere to his dress code when he was the one who insisted in the first place that people come as they were. According to the story, the poor guest who was thus confronted was unable to answer, as he was dumbfounded. Most of us would be as well if this happened to us. The nobleman had his mind made up as to the image he wanted his wedding festivities to reflect, so he instructed his servants to bind the unwelcomed guest by the hands and feet and throw him out.

Looking beneath the surface of this story for the spiritual reality captured here, I interpret the wedding feast as the Wedding Feast of the Son of Man. It is the Wedding Feast of the Mystical Marriage. A wedding feast is symbolic of many things simultaneously — a coming of age (or rite of passage, as the anthropologist would say), a celebration, a consummation, a union, an alliance between different elements, and so on. The fact that the original list of guests refused to attend suggests that these people had their own celebrations, each his own thing going on. This is addressing a very human condition in our approach to spiritual practice.

In the traditional approach to spiritual practice, almost everyone has loyalty to a prior commitment and becomes incapable of recognizing that for which he is supposedly striving. Many of us do not realize that all our personal realizations and celebrations must take a backseat to a greater realization and celebration. This is the realization and celebration of our Collective Becoming, our coming of age as a species.

The guests who were initially invited represent our various religious and esoteric traditions. The invitation, in a way, was an encounter with the object of their search. But the fact that they refused to go suggests that many of these traditions, religions, and paths have become sidetracked from the real purpose for which they exist and thus end in themselves.

In the terms of reference of the parable, this is why the nobleman expected them to come to the wedding feast of his son. This suggests to us that all religions and esoteric traditions must learn to defer to the Grand Realization represented by our Collective Transformation, our coming of age, our New-Collective-Consensus Reality, which is symbolically represented as the Wedding Feast of the Son of Man. Each of us must pour the results of our individual realizations into this Grand Realization. Life for each of us must not stop with our personal spiritual enlightenment. Personal realization must be followed by efforts to bring about the enlightenment of the whole of humanity. We must endeavor to establish externally the Truth we have realized within.

Undertaking to commit oneself to the service of humanity is necessary on account of the changing nature of spiritual realization. Realization is really a moving target. In the parable, no one is excluded from the Wedding Feast. Wherever one is, one qualifies to participate in the Grand Realization. But there is a catch! We have to make ourselves worthy of the invitation. We must have a "garment" fitting to the occasion, and this garment is purity of heart. It is every individual's reasonable duty to have an open and pure heart. That is how we get the ability to recognize that for which we are striving. This is why an invitation to the Wedding Feast does not absolve one of the responsibility to be personally prepared.

In the context of our everyday reality, an invitation to the Wedding Feast means that some of us may be exposed to spontaneous spiritual experiences and mystical states of consciousness as a matter of Grace. But even so, we cannot leave it at that and fail to develop our beings. A spontaneous experience does not necessarily mean we are developed spiritually any more than a failure to have extraordinary experiences can be interpreted as a lack of spiritual development. All that a spontaneous experience suggests is that we were in a position to receive God's Grace — like the ship that was fortunate enough to have its sails trained to the wind. After we have been touched by a mystical experience, we must prove ourselves worthy of it by bringing the rest of our life up to a level where such experiences become natural to us.

As we continue to explore the parable, we might be tempted to think that it does not make much of a difference to the guest who was cast out, because he was on the street to begin with anyway. To look at it in this fashion would be to miss the message this parable is conveying to us. When we are called into the Wedding Feast we become aware of higher things, of which we had no previous notion. So to be thrust back into the former life hurts. It hurts to know that one had a chance at something significant but could not take advantage of it. That is why one is worse off for not having a wedding garment, because it is really a small price to pay for having been accorded so high an honor.

While we are on the subject, I feel that I should say something about the role of organized religion in the context of our New-Consciousness-Reality. We saw in this parable that the invitees on the initial guest list refused to attend the wedding feast. I feel strongly that this is directly addressing the role of organized religion. Organized religion has done more to keep us out of the Wedding Feast of our Collective Becoming than any other single factor on the earth. That is why, I believe, that in a New Age[4] context, organized religion would not function as it has up to now, because the premise of religion would have to change to accommodate a changed human nature. This changed nature would have reclaimed most of the qualities we now project outside of ourselves onto God. Consequently, the exercise of responsibility towards our world and each other, the capacity to care and love, and to think objectively, would be expressions of this new nature. Only then, I believe, will we express true humanity.

The proper role of religion in our life should be to help us to create and preserve within ourselves a certain Sacred Space reserved for future use.[5] In its proper place, religion allows us to pay tribute to the possibility of entertaining reverence and wholeness in our lives on an everyday basis. However, more often than not, religion ends up having us hope for a better life somewhere else. The New Age is a time when ancient promises can be fulfilled, when that Sacred Space in reserve can be filled. When this Space has been filled with a sense of wholeness that attests to our unity and the unity of all life, then the Master that has been promised by the various religions will have returned. The religious experience in its purity is therefore not a matter of doctrinal truth, but one of surrendering to this sense of wholeness that attests to the unity of Life.

IS SUFFERING NECESSARY?

Is suffering the antithesis of Realization? One encounters in various quarters the notion that suffering is the result of some sort of failure on the part of the seeker. This idea holds that suffering results from a person's inability to see the greater good that the situation he may be involved in is leading to. From the perspective on transformation we have pursued so far, suffering stands right at the center of the enigma of this world and is not so easily explained away. Our first step in gaining a perspective on suffering is to realize that suffering is not homogeneous. Sometimes it is necessary that we experience some degree of personal suffering before we come to an understanding of its place in spiritual work.

There was a period of my life when I felt so devastated that I thought I had touched bottom. The event that was most inconceivable and most feared was actually happening to me: My wife of four years left without advance warning, taking our baby daughter who had held my heart captive for the eleven months she had been part of my life. The first few days and weeks were unbearable. I prayed to, pleaded with, argued at, and finally tried to bargain with God. My agony was intensified as none of my closest friends were around to share my burden. For some inexplicable reason, my closest and most trusted friends happened to be thousands of miles away at the time. I was totally alone. It was time for me to rediscover God!

During one very intense session of prayers and tears, I decided to consult an "oracle." The only one I knew was in the form of a game that my brothers and sisters and I played during childhood. We would open the Bible at random and read the passage that fell under the right thumb. Back then, we were doing it for fun, but now I was grasping at anything that would shed light on my present predicament. As the Bible opened, my right thumb fell on a passage in II Samuel. I read a sufficient number of verses before and ahead of this passage to get the context.

The gist of what I read was this: David, the king, had incurred God's wrath by taking a census of the Israelites in disobedience to a divine command. As punishment, a seer by the name of Gad was sent to David to present him with three different tribulations from which he must choose on behalf of the Israelites. These were a famine, an invasion, and an epidemic. David chose the epidemic because he foresaw that it would be of short duration and would thus cause the least hardship. When the epidemic was over, he decided to build an altar to make burnt offerings in thanksgiving. His seer, Gad, told him of a location that was appropriate for the burnt offering. This was the threshing floor of one by the name of Araunah. King David went in person to Araunah with an offer to purchase the threshing floor and the necessary oxen for the burnt offering. Araunah, upon hearing that the king wanted to purchase his threshing floor and his oxen, offered them to him free of cost. To this rather kind offer, David replied that he would not make burnt offerings to the Lord God of that which did not cost him anything.

Here was my answer! I quickly realized that my suffering was the price that I must pay to offer my life to God! It is so easy for us to offer ourselves to God when we feel that God is being gracious toward us. But how about when things are not going so well? This lesson was all that I needed to pull myself together. If David was not going to offer a sacrifice to his God that did not cost him anything, neither was I.

That incident was over fifteen years ago, and today my perspective has broadened to include additional insights as to the role of suffering in spiritual work.

PERSPECTIVES ON SUFFERING

From my perspective, suffering can be classified into at least four categories: involuntary, voluntary, dispensational, and developmental.

Involuntary Suffering

Involuntary suffering includes most ordinary forms of suffering. It is this form that people usually think about when they say that suffering is self-induced or self-inflicted. This category of suffering can include almost anything in the range of the frustration of an unfulfilled desire to reaping the consequences of some past indiscretion. Here, the role of suffering is to get one to adjust the orientation of one's life and relationships.

Voluntary Suffering

Voluntary suffering results when we undergo hardships with the hope of securing some long-term benefits. Thus, we may decide to forego present satisfaction to wrestle with a bad habit, to learn a new skill, to give birth to a vision — with the risk of being misunderstood. In general, voluntary suffering occurs when we leave the familiar for the unfamiliar.

Dispensational Suffering

This category of suffering occurs in the form of accidents, natural disasters, and the like. Individuals so affected might not be individually liable, apart from being at a particular place at a particular time or sharing group values and the like. Usually, one can find several persons in such a situation of suffering who could have avoided a particular fate had they listened to their own inner guidance. In this sense, this form of suffering results more from inaction than action.

Developmental Suffering

Developmental suffering occurs in the sense that as the human reality moves to broader horizons, a certain widening and deepening of our consciousness must take place. It is neither voluntary nor involuntary. In the sense that transformation involves the intermingling of different levels of reality, various adjustments at the human level are necessary in very much the same way that we must dig a foundation for a building. The taller the building, the deeper must be its foundation; an individual with great developmental potential, if that is to flower in a spiritual context, would have to "suffer a little while" so that he can come to know the depth and breadth of the human experience as well as its heights. Suffering in this context occurs as we die to the known to create room for the Unknowable to manifest itself.

It is this kind of suffering which the mystics have labeled the *dark night of the Soul.* Before I became aware of this term I referred to its manifestation in my own life as "the departure of my Guardian Angel." I could just as easily have called it the death of God.

Dark Night of the Soul

When we are awakening into spiritual consciousness, we will usually find that we are caught between two worlds. There is the "old world" with its tried and true formulas — with its proven techniques. It is a world that may be comfortable and relatively secure, though cramped by paradoxes and contradictions. Then there is the "new world" which demands to be born in our consciousness. It is a world whose secrets have not yet been systematized in formulas and techniques, and whose boundaries are not yet clearly defined. This world is full of risks. It is also demanding of our openness, our trust: we feel vulnerable in it for it offers no guarantees save that of allowing us to see and be more of what we really are. It is logical — in the sense of the logic of the "old world" — that when faced with the choice of living according to the principles of the newer versus the older world, we often want to remain with the old: "Better the devil you know than one you don't know," as the saying goes. This is the time when Divine influence intervenes to wean us from the breasts of the Divine Mother. For unless we are pushed, our awakening falters. In cultures where breast-feeding is prevalent, a mother may wean her infant at the stage where it is capable of digesting stronger food by putting a bitter, though harmless substance on her nipples. The infant child now must turn from one source of nourishment to another.

With the process of spiritual awakening, the moment of turning from one level of relationship to Existence to another comes when we develop the capacity to see our many possibilities for a fuller relationship with Life. As long as we are capable of seeing these possibilities we are capable of embodying them. Unfortunately, we may not realize this and insist on retaining a relationship to Existence that is more appropriate for the spiritual infant.

THE DEATH OF GOD

Although I was quite spontaneous in my assessment of the period of unprecedented difficulties in my life as the departure of my Guardian Angel, my designation was a metaphor for what happens when we are forced to internalize processes we previously attributed to an external agent. Usually, we appeal to a supernatural agent when the affairs of our life are not going according to our expectations, and quite often we seem to get results as a direct response to our appeals or prayers. This was true of my own life experience until my own *dark night*. God ceased to be a reality I could manipulate, consciously or unconsciously.

In a psychological sense, the departure of my Guardian Angel meant that my link to God was terminated at the level of my familiar orientation to Reality. This required me to strive to reestablish this link on a higher level, on another dimension. When the Existentialist philosophers talk about the death of God, I believe they are pointing at something similar. As a matter of fact, anyone who experiences growth in the transformational sense must experience the death of God at several levels. In reality, it is not God that dies, but our projections on God that must dissolve — dissipate like an apparition — if we are to grow in responsibility in a universal sense.

THE OTHER SIDE OF THE ABYSS: ENLIGHTENMENT

There is a point at which, after a period of purgation and suffering, we may arrive at a stage where it is possible to redefine the totality of our relationships with the world at large. The basis of this new web of relationships lies in a new sense of identity that is based on a continuity of being and existence with the rest of the Universe. This stage of the transformational journey marks what can be called enlightenment. The key to enlightenment lies in a deconditioning of our perception of reality. In a way, our awareness of reality becomes unscrambled. Previously, our sense of reality was based on viewing Life from the vantage point of a separate ego, but now the perspective is broadened to include more than a personal point of view.

Prior to the enlightened state, our view of the world is constrained by our personal point of view on the world. A "point of view" is just that. It is a perspective from a certain vantage point. This vantage point usually excludes all that is not in our interest. But since what we perceive as our interest is only determined by one small aspect of the Self, this perception confines Reality only to what is in the interest of this small aspect, namely, the ego. Enlightenment, on the other hand, requires that we do not confine perception to the ego, but to all of the Self.

When we have lost the need for an ordinary perception of the world, we cease to be insular. The suffering of the world becomes ours, its joys and accomplishments, ours. When misfortunes come, we have the assurance that they will eventually pass away. When glad tidings come, we acknowledge also that these too will pass. The mind now functions as a witness to the flow of Life.

We do not experience enlightenment as a result of applying techniques. It happens on its own when we have demonstrated in our beings that we no longer have a need for an ordinary perception of the world. Furthermore, the ordinary mind in its usual mode of functioning is not compatible with enlightenment as a state of being. When we are in the ordinary mind and are confronted with something unpleasant, we recoil. We cry "Why me? Why me?" We are fearful and feel offended by pain and hardship. Those are all right for others but not for us. By rejecting our share of the difficulties of the world, we are placing more validity on what we have individually experienced as contrasted to what the rest of humanity has experienced and is experiencing. Functioning in the ordinary mind, we consciously accept only that reality which is compatible with what we desire.

The onset of enlightenment may be paradoxical on account of its being characterized not by knowledge, but by lack of it. We may feel totally cut off from all that we know, such that we might feel like a child. The only thing of which we can be certain at this stage is that we know nothing for certain. However, we soon find that in this state of unknowing we are one with all.

The first manifestation of the enlightened state in our psyche is in making certain commitments irrevocable regarding our relationship to the whole of life. Certain ideas we previously found difficult to express now become effortless. They become an expression of our being. But at the same time, other things that were previously easy become difficult. Most of the things that are written about the enlightened state discuss only the side of this reality where life becomes a flow, where life is spontaneous. Buried under this spontaneous flow is the side that is difficult. It is difficult because it calls for a mobilization and marshalling of our energies to enable us to actively participate in the process which, at the same time, we are immersed in. The difficulty stems from our new responsibilities as co-creators in the process of Life. Creativity in this sense requires that we bring newness into daily life. The difficulty we experience at first occurs because we do not have anyone to emulate. Previously, we were satisfied to allow ourselves to be carried by trends and events, but now we realize that we have the power to create our own reality. Our awareness is now in its unscrambled state — in its bare essence — freedom and responsibility.

Notes, Chapter 12

1. I was discussing the principle behind this story with a friend, and with a touch of humor she placed the whole thing in perspective by remarking that, after thousands of years, lentils are still cheap.
2. It is important that this point is not misinterpreted. In light of the spiritual principles we are espousing, there must be integrity in everything we do — outer and inner must harmonize. However, concerning material success, we must not expect correspondence between the two levels.

3. As our aspirations increase, we penetrate deeper into the Mystery of life, which renders all our past achievements and accomplishments pale and insignificant compared to spiritual participation in life. The deeper we penetrate the Mystery, the lesser is our need to derive personal compensation (whether subtle or gross) for being engaged in the spiritual life.

4. I use the term "New Age" specifically in the context of a higher level of individual and collective human consciousness. This will be characterized by an increased sensitivity to Life and to each other.

5. In the sense of a collective rather than individual or ego-directed use.

13   The Transformational Life

As more and more people become aware of our potential for spiritual advancement, we hear much talk of the "Aquarian Conspiracy," about "paradigm shift," about transformation and conscious evolution, about Spirit of Resurgence, New Age, and other exotic terms. However, despite outward signs of transformational awareness, the fundamental question we must each ask ourselves is this: *How have we really changed, apart from acquiring a new vocabulary of words and concepts?* We must look for the "bottom line" of our transformation. We need to know what, if anything, has precipitated in our beings after reading all those books, attending all those workshops, listening to all those lectures, doing all those hours of meditation.

For some of us, our interest in transformation seems to go through a honeymoon period after which our lives return to their old prosaic regularity, rooted in the old values, old alliances, old fears, old priorities. Somewhere along the line something refused to budge. The sun of the "New Dawn" failed to rise above the horizon. We give in to panic, wondering whether what we thought to be dawn really wasn't dusk; whether sunrise really wasn't sunset. We fear that we may have lost ground in the world as we allowed ourselves to become sidetracked by the esoteric. We may even play down our fears, consoling ourselves that maybe all is not lost; we have discovered some sense of purpose, the proof of which is evident in our newfound concepts. Also, we discover that we are not as hard-headed, thick-skinned, or hard-nosed as before. No matter that we conduct our lives in essentially the same manner as before, we assure ourselves that things are now done for a better reason, or reasons congruent with the paradigms of the New Age. So we continue to seek power, believing that we no longer seek it for its own sake, but to disperse it. We seek wealth and fame, perhaps even more ardently than before, but we tell ourselves we no longer seek it for its own sake, but for independence and financial autonomy so that we are better positioned to do what we can to hasten the New Age. Never mind that we reinforce "Old Age" values while we are doing so.

The truth of the matter is that many of us on the transformational path succumb to the *Tonight's Dinner Syndrome* but may not want to admit it to ourselves. Let me relate a story to explain what the Tonight's Dinner Syndrome is. This tale is attributed to Gurdjieff and is retold by Ouspensky in his book *In Search of the Miraculous*.[1]

As the tale goes, there once lived a wolf who stole a great many sheep and reduced local residents to many hardships and tears. For some unknown reason, the wolf suddenly felt qualms of conscience and began to repent for his misdeeds. He made the difficult decision to reform and not slaughter any more sheep. In order to do this seriously, he went to the local church and asked the priest for a blessing. Since the priest as well had lost many sheep to the wolf, he was particularly intent on ensuring that the prayers were effective. Consequently, the service ran very long. Suddenly, the wolf looked through a window and saw that sheep were being driven home for the night. He began to fidget, but the priest went on and on, without end. At last, the wolf could contain himself no longer and he shouted, "Finish it priest! Or all the sheep will be driven home and I'll be left without tonight's dinner!"

Here, in the wolf's attitude, is the story of us all, at least many of us. We are always ready to throw caution to the wind to usher in the New Age, to become stewards and ambassadors of the New Consciousness, to build the New Heaven and New Earth. But Tonight's Dinner is another matter. As Gurdjieff commented, "A man always wishes to begin with something big. But this is impossible; there can be no choice, we must begin with things of today."[2]

I wholeheartedly agree with Gurdjieff that we must begin with small things, immediate things. This is where the real battle is fought and won. This is the real transformation. Let the paradigms shift where they may and the Aquarian Conspiracy transpire where it must. Transformation is not a matter of concepts. It takes place at the level where life itself is lived, in the home, in the marketplace, in the workplace, on the street, in traffic, over the telephone, in relationship with one's spouse, children, parents, neighbor.

Transformation is you and me, as we feel for each other, look out for each other, create opportunities for and with each other, share with each other, hurt for each other, rejoice with each other. That which we try to capture in exotic concepts is nothing more than good old-fashioned caring. As we learn to care, all the wishful things we have been talking about and to which we have given exotic names will fall into place, fall into their own. Unless we become attuned to this "bottom line" of our transformation, the reality of Tonight's Dinner will always draw us back to our former states of being, our untransformed selves unembellished with fancy words and concepts. That is why, in our moments of crises when we are tested and tried, all the concepts we have accumulated, all the meditation we have done, and God knows what else, do not seem to help. The only thing that will help is our built-in sense of care and involvement. As Laotzu said so well, "The invincible shield of caring is a weapon from the sky against being dead."[3]

The fruit of our transformation is therefore Love in action, or our unity in expression. Perhaps, if we are deeply concerned about transformation, we won't mind foregoing Tonight's Dinner. And ironically, it is in such moments when we are called to make sacrifices that transformation is found waiting for us to encounter it.

LOVE: THE ULTIMATE SPIRITUAL PRACTICE

As I have more and more occasion to speak to individuals and groups on transformational themes, I am often asked what kind of daily spiritual practice I engage in. My answer to this question is that I practice LOVE. In the sense that I use it, Love is equanimity. It is a composite of steadiness of purpose, openness to what Life has to offer, sensitivity to the presence and needs of others, effort with patience, and a willingness to make sacrifices. In this sense, it is the ultimate spiritual technique, though beyond technique. To attune oneself to Love is to attune oneself to God, to the Energy that holds the Universe together. This is why Love is the ultimate technique; if we can attune ourselves to Love in this physical dimension, we become attuned to Love everywhere else that Love is observed. That way, we use Love as a "carrier wave" to expand our consciousness. We cease to be separate, cease to feel insignificant, cease to feel disinherited and disenfranchised. When we commit ourselves to expressing Love, we become known to God. Because in expressing Love, God in turn will be expressing His Being through us.

The advantage of this type of spiritual practice is that it can be conducted everywhere, in our jobs, in relationships, in the marketplace, in meditation. At the start of the day we rehearse how we are going to give expression to Love, at the end of the day we reflect on whether we succeeded in expressing Love. In relating to others, we try to see in them the same principle that holds the Universe together, and we try to relate to this principle in them even though they may rub us the wrong way. In the marketplace we strive for fairness, knowing that only in fairness is the one principle that unites us all celebrated. In meditation we try to ascend to greater heights of Love, greater degrees of unity of purpose and will with the Universe. We descend or emerge from our meditation with a desire to assimilate and disperse this Love. In prayer we try to acknowledge this Love, to pledge our allegiance to *It*, to elevate *It*, to renew our acceptance of *It*.

By degrees, or quite suddenly, as It may please, this Love may alight and nest in our hearts because It knows that It is welcome there, that It has a home there. More than anything else, this Love seeks to be affirmed in our daily lives. It wants to incarnate more and more of Itself in matter. Our entire life should be dedicated to facilitating this process.

To live the transformational life is to be fully engaged in creating the right conditions for the spiritual to manifest to a greater and greater degree. The transformational life is lived on the conviction that the True Life, or Reality, can be found here. And rightly so. For if we live on the assumption that life is real somewhere else and not here, what is to say when we get "There," where it is supposedly real, that we will not contaminate it there also and rob it of its Reality?

The transformational life endeavors to find the formula that makes this present reality Real. Perhaps, that is the only way that we can experience Reality elsewhere too. Perhaps, once we've found the formula, it operates on every dimension, like a master key! Spiritual work should therefore be something that we are prepared to devote our entire life to, not something we do for a particular result, then discard afterwards. In this effort, everything else pales in significance, even religion. Religion mostly seeks to escape the enigma of this world. In contrast, what the transformational life is seeking is a way of life that unravels this enigma. This is done when we each find within ourselves the formula that reconciles Earth and Heaven. When this formula is found, we will not be satisfied with wanting to ascend to Heaven; we will also see the possibility and the need to bring Heaven to Earth. The unity of Earth and Heaven is not something that can be dogmatically asserted. It is something to be personally realized in our consciousness.

It is important that we do not mistake complacency for equanimity. With complacency, we are blind to opportunities to bring meaning to life situations. With equanimity, our ability to reconcile opposites and conflicts within ourselves helps to detoxify situations that would normally sap our energy.

Equanimity, as a spiritual practice, also provides us with an acid test with which to evaluate diverse spiritual techings: *Does this teaching assist me in finding meaning in earth-life, or is it asking me to believe that the True Life is to be found elsewhere, in some ethereal dimension?* With equanimity, or Love, at the core of our spiritual practice, our credo becomes: "As above so below." If God is to be found anywhere, God must be found here too! If God can't be found here, then God can't be found anywhere. There are no techniques that can teach us how to find God here on earth; only patient and loving attunement of our consciousness to our unity and interconnectedness can do this.

VALUES OF THE TRANSFORMED HUMAN

Those of us who become aware of our possibilities and begin to embody Life and Consciousness in greater degrees than we have previously will have an impact on our human nature and the way we collectively perceive reality. Eventually, this will lead to a change in our relationships and the institutions that support these redefined relationships. As they presently function, our institutions and relationships are involved in an infinite loop of mutual reinforcement. Since they are rooted in an understanding of reality as defined by an ego-centered consciousness, they function to sustain and reinforce the ego-centered consciousness that created them.

For many years now, I have been intrigued by the possibilities of a transformed human community that would result from a transformed human nature. This has not been merely out of armchair curiosity, but out of a desire to cooperate as much as possible with such possibilities as they are sighted. If we can intuit how society would behave and interact when transformation has occurred on a large scale, that insight could help us to speed up the transformational process itself at the personal and collective levels. We can each uphold the values and put the support systems in place that would abet and reinforce these transformed values.

I have always found such an exercise difficult. It is hard to predict how one person, much less the whole human society, will change and adjust to challenges. Add to this the explosion of creativity that would result from unleashed brain potential (particularly of the right brain variety), and our surmises would be equivalent to looking through the wrong end of a telescope. I believe the best we can do under these circumstances is to proceed in a step-by-step manner.

- First, we need to look at all the factors that characterize an ego-centered consciousness and treat each one as a constraint that is blocking the manifestation of a transformed human community.

- The next step is to mentally remove these constraints one at a time to see how our relationships will change in their absence.

- The third step is to derive implications for the new institutions that would arise from these changed relationships.

- Fourth, we must "sponsor" each aspect of our changed future by living at this present moment as if that future, with its changed relationships and new human consciousness, were already a reality.

This last step is the crux of the transformational life, for it calls forth the highest we have to offer as individuals through our faculties of intellect, feelings, and will.

The values that will result in a transformed human community will arise from transformations of our human intellect, feelings, and will. At present, our human faculties of intellect, feelings, and will function defectively: greed and self-interest have impaired the capacity of the intellect for objective and impartial judgment; fear, self-love, and envy have all but destroyed our capacity for genuine and sincere feelings; competitiveness and a sense of separativeness have atrophied our sense of purpose and personal responsibility. The restoration of these faculties would mean the generation of values that would provide guidelines for meaningful living.

An objective and impartial intellect would mean the restoration of our ability to determine our needs from our wants. It would also help us to understand our place in the scheme of Nature. A restored capacity to feel deeply and sincerely will enable us to have concern for others and to value for others what we value for ourselves. This also implies the inability to hurt, to deprive, or to exploit others without immediately experiencing the consequences at a feeling level. When we've restored our will, we will learn how to tap inner abilities and creativity, and thus become capable of motivating ourselves to work without the enticement of rewards. Personal success will then be defined in terms of how much we contribute to the well-being of others.

The beauty of this vision of a transformed human is that it lies within our capability. Actually, some of us already claim these faculties under pretense, and as we well know, we can only counterfeit an article or a quality if the real thing already exists.

THE NEXT STEP — LIVING OUR TRANSFORMED VALUES

The more I think about it, the more I am convinced that the New Consciousness we seek to embody has its own agenda. And not only that, it is relentless and irrepressible in the pursuit of this agenda. In this regard it is like a flood, and like one will cut its own channel to its destination unless one is provided for it. This holds true at both the collective and individual levels of existence. If we are convinced that our individual lives are not ends in themselves, we must then begin to query what the agenda of Life is and commit ourselves to meeting it. Only then can we fulfill our transformational potential of becoming receptacles and conduits of Divine Energies.

During the earlier stages of my awakening process I used to have a recurring dream. In the dream I would find myself seated in an examination room waiting for the examination paper. As I waited I would realize that not only was I not prepared, I did not know what subject matter I was to be tested on. At first I would awake from this dream anxious and frustrated. Eventually I learned what the dream was communicating to me: *I must meet Life on its own terms — in the moment!* The dreams stopped after I got that message.

To meet Life in the moment means that we must put aside our own agendas in preference for fulfilling the agenda of Life. We must query constantly what Life requires of us in every situation, not what we want from Life. For each of us, the *next step* we must take to fulfill our transformational potential is that of accomplishing what Life requires of us *right now* — not tomorrow, not next year, not after we've received a revelation, but this moment . . . and the next! At a practical level this commitment will require us to live a life of *embodied spirituality* — a life of integrity, where the principles we profess are expressed in our activities until they become instinctual, part of our nature.

To this point, I have shared insights and perspectives with you that I have distilled out of my own life experience. If, as a result of this sharing, I have in any small way contributed to an increase in the intensity of your aspirations or inspired you to travel your own path more courageously, I would consider my effort a success and my own journey validated. For me, the transformational impulse does not come to an abrupt end with our individual glimpses into our possibilities. It now faces the more challenging task of getting us to seek out and find our collective possibilities. It is only with this second task that the first will have any meaning.

I would like you to pause for a moment and do the following exercise:

> Take a few deep breaths and go within. Ask yourself the following: *"Where am I at this moment on the transformational journey? And what is the next step I must take on this journey?"*

Your answers to these questions contain all the revelation you will ever need to propel you on the journey! It does not matter how modest the effort seems: No step is too small, no effort inconsequential. Indeed, Life is *faithful* and will respond to every sincere aspiration we have and honest effort we make. Once we see this we will also see how all of our living becomes a prayer that will be answered. In other words, we can use our living as an *invocation*. Our aspirations, intentions, values, beliefs, thoughts and actions are component parts of this invocation.

With the assurance that Life will fulfill its part of the bargain, all we need concern ourselves about, to progress on the transformational path, is our own sincerity and faithfulness.

As we take leave of each other let us hope and pray that the symphony of our collective aspirations and interlocking lives charms to earth our Collective Future — a future that already exists.

Notes, Chapter 13

1. P. D. Ouspensky, *In Search of the Miraculous* (New York: Harcourt Brace Jovanovich, 1949), 366.
2. Ibid., 366.
3. Witter Bynner (translater), *The Way of Life According to Laotzu* (New York: Capricorn Books, 1962), 69.

APPENDIX
A Transformational Workshop:
Navigating the Path of Process

OVERVIEW

This appendix integrates the many layers of information found in the body of this book. It lays out a practical framework that can be used as a context for one's personal transformational work. It is organized with two basic aims in mind: first, to assist us in developing clarity about our spiritual aims and objectives, and second, to present a conceptual overview that can assist us in connecting the many aspects of our spiritual seeking and expression into one integrative framework.

The following diagram contains, in a schematic way, some of the key transformational steps found in the body of this book. The idea behind it is to allow us to place ourselves in the picture and evaluate our development as we move along. I recommend that the reader work with this diagram a number of times. The premise behind this exercise is that each time we work with it we will learn something new about ourselves and, more importantly, develop some clarity as to what we can do to further deepen our consciousness. Working with this diagram has the potential to become a meditation and a device to help us to focus our energies at the mental and emotional levels.

THE DIAGRAM

The diagram is divided into four zones, each one representing a different level of relationship to Life. Zone one represents uncon-

NAVIGATING THE PATH OF PROCESS

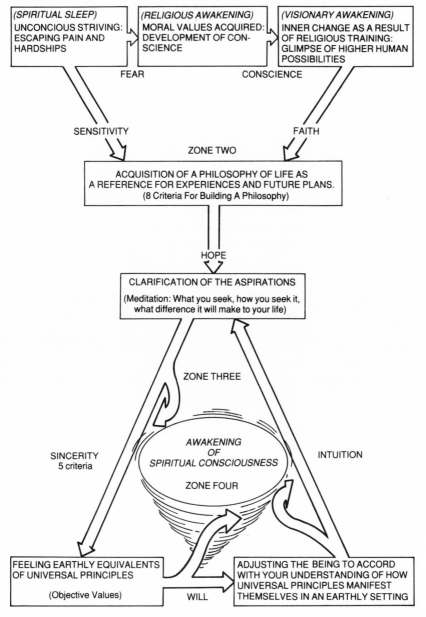

scious striving; zone two, conscious striving; zone three, organic change in one's being; and zone four, the awakening of spiritual consciousness.

ZONE ONE: UNCONSCIOUS STRIVING

There are three boxes in zone one, representing three states of human consciousness:

- a state of spiritual sleep
- a state of awakened religious sentiment
- a state of visionary awakening

Normally, as we develop spiritually, we progress laterally from spiritual sleep to visionary awakening.

In the first box, an individual's reality is dominated by duality, characterized by the pursuit of happiness. As a result, such an individual is focused on escaping pain and hardships. The view of reality that predominates is that of alienation and separation, and therefore competition. All the striving that we express here is unconscious in the sense that we expend our energy trying to fill various needs as they arise in us. Usually, the way that we progress out of this stage is through some form of moral discipline, as in various forms of established religion. The motivation to undertake such a discipline may be provided by fear of the unknown, of death, of "the wrath of God."

This path of development is not the only one available, for if we are sensitive enough, we can move directly to the second level of striving, conscious striving, but more about this later.

The second box represents the stage of trying to come to terms with the objective world of other people. Here, the goal is to acquire a system for determining appropriate behavior, namely, a system of morality. As we practice such values, we develop conscience. With conscience, we are able to feel for another person and are able to take our places as responsible members of the human community. It is only now that we stop perceiving life from a sense of identity defined by separation (i.e., the "I" cut off from everything else).

With the faculty of conscience, we begin to ask the "big questions" — questions leading to an understanding of Life as a principle.

The third box represents visionary awakening. Visionary awakening is experienced as a result of inner change taking place in us as a consequence of practicing ethical values. This is the beginning of a visionary or farsighted outlook on life.

As we enter the stage of visionary awakening we begin to acquire spiritual goals. Usually these goals are formulated and given verbal expression in terms relevant to the society in which we live. Here we begin to intuit the meaning of human experience on earth. This stage is the very threshold of spiritual consciousness, for it is here that we start to accept responsibility for ourselves. As a result of being able to intuit the purpose of human existence, we also begin to formulate ideas about the ideal state of human society. This visionary exercise bestows personal benefits on us, for in so doing, we develop an understanding of our own spiritual possibilities.

These states of conscious spiritual sleep, religious awakening, and visionary awakening are not mutually exclusive. We can have a consciousness where the dominant mode of being is the seeking of pleasure but may have moments and patches of religious sentience and visionary fervor. This is quite common and can lead to an unbalanced personality when the visionary fervor is not supported by some basic orientation in ethics.

THE PASSAGE FROM UNCONSCIOUS TO CONSCIOUS STRIVING

Faith

We move from zone one to two, and therefore from unconscious to conscious striving, as a result of the quality of being known as Faith. *Faith is a willingness to commit ourselves to the principles necessary to make our vision of humanity a reality. Faith allows us to live beyond time-space limitations.*

Sensitivity

Earlier, we stated that sensitivity enables one to go directly from a consciousness of separation to conscious striving. *Sensitivity is an awareness of cause and effect, of motives and the impulses that drive us.* Generally, it means having objective knowledge of oneself. Self-knowledge is obtained from noncritical self-observation, from analysis, and from examining how we feel about the "big questions."

An Exercise in Self-Awareness

The following set of questions is an exercise to bring to the surface some of the assumptions we might have about transformation. Indirectly, it is an exercise in self-awareness. I recommend that the exercise be done by two or more individuals, each person responding verbally to the questions as they are put to him or her by another.

1. Do you consider your life full right now? If not, what do you consider to be missing? How critical is the missing element and how far will you go to secure it? If your life is full, what factors have been most essential in contributing to this fullness?
2. What annoys you most about people? What do you like most about people? Is it possible that these feelings have anything to do with the way you feel about yourself?
3. What do you consider to have been your peak spiritual experience? What spiritual experience would you like to attain by the end of your physical life?
4. How important is formal religion to you? Have you ever changed or contemplated changing your religion? What are the reasons for which you will change or refuse to change your religion?
5. What is the most important thing in your life right now? What are the most time-consuming things in your life right now? List your activities and interests in terms of the amount of time you spend on them. How urgent is it to you that you organize your life in terms of your deeper interests?

6. What does the term "spiritual realization" mean to you? Which of the following statements most closely reflects the true meaning of spiritual transformation as you conceive it? Rank in descending order, 1 as closest, 2 next closest, etc.
   Spiritual Transformation is:
   (a) Our ability to see and derive new meaning in religious symbols and expressions;
   (b) A movement into the unknown, where it is easier to know what you must leave behind than what you can secure for yourself;
   (c) An extension of human faculties and abilities;
   (d) The progressive realization and nurturance into expression of one's true, essential being or identity;
   (e) A return to less complex, life-enhancing modes of being and living;
   (f) The education of the various parts of one's being with the ideals of the Spirit, the most essential being a realization of our unity at all levels of existence.
   Clue: Consider differences between cause and effect of a transformed consciousness; also between process and technique.
7. Connect all six statements according to your ranking and write a short essay reflecting how you understand the transformational process.

   After the above has been completed, replace all references to the second and third person (one's, your, etc.) with the first person (I, my, etc.).

Acquiring Self-Knowledge

There are many routes to self-knowledge. The immediate goal of self-knowledge is self-acceptance. For people who can afford it, psychoanalysis has been a well-trodden road. For the average person, there is a quicker, less expensive, and even more effective path that, if properly utilized, can lead to the same ends. This is astrological analysis. I will suggest that those who would like to pursue this avenue shop around for a highly recommended astrologer who emphasizes the psychological/spiritual approach and have him or her do a personal horoscope. The process should be repeated three to six months later with another astrologer and particular attention should be paid to factors that repeat themselves. We should seek to discover the following through astrological analysis:

- The life purpose as expressed in the chart.

- The Life calling, or the activities that may facilitate the actualization of one's life purpose.

- Strengths and undeveloped talents that may be utilized in the service of realizing one's life purpose.

- Problems areas that one should be aware of and the means of resolving them.

- Crisis points in the life and their general psychological and spiritual nature.

This insight from astrology should form the seed from which we can continue self-discovery through our own ongoing analysis and observation. I would like to offer a strong word of caution against the use of astrology as a crutch, to justify oneself or for the prediction of events. Such uses have the opposite result of retarding self-knowledge and development.

ZONE TWO: CONSCIOUS STRIVING

Conscious striving begins only after we have obtained a certain degree of self-knowledge. It is only then that we are ready to get a coherent perspective on life. This perspective is also called a philosophy of life.

A philosophy of Life is a framework that allows us to accept life and merge with it, as opposed to fighting with it. A philosophy of life is equivalent to cleansing the lens of the mind. We begin to develop a philosophy with answers we settle on as a consequence of asking the questions of life, for example: *Is there purpose to life? What shall I make the target of striving in my life? How can we make a difference to the world for having been born into it?* and so on.

Below is a set of pointers that may be useful as we go about putting together a philosophy of life.

Pointers on Developing a Philosophy

1. Reading biographies of people we admire, to find out what were the challenges of their lives and how they mastered them. We should look for the principles that were instrumental in sculpting their lives.

2. Doing a comparative study of the key ideas of major world religions (e.g., Judaism, Christianity, Islam, Hinduism, Buddhism, Taoism). What do they identify as the purpose of human life on earth? How do they account for evil? What prescription do they offer for a fulfilled life?

3. Doing a mental assessment of the adjustments we would have to make in our lives if we adopt a certain idea as part of the repertoire of our philosophy.

4. Doing an inventory of all the beliefs that we hold, examining each one in light of our own personal experiences and in the context of other principles we have already validated in our own lives. What rationale can we find for continuing to subscribe to a belief that does not fall in line with what we know for sure?

5. We must try to see our lives as an "influence" which comes into the world and leaves at a certain point. How have we affected the world for having been a part of it? Is there any specific way that we would want to be remembered? What changes do we have to make to our lives to ensure that we are remembered the way we hope to be?

The eight criteria discussed in Chapter 4 can be regarded as a touchstone; that is, when we come into contact with a particular idea or doctrine or world view, we can run it through the eight checks mentioned in this chapter. Again, these criteria are:

Relevance	Consanguinity
Pertinence	Congruence
Continuity	Verifiability
Intentionality	Objectivity

MOVING FROM CONSCIOUS STRIVING OF THE MENTAL VARIETY TO CONSCIOUS STRIVING OF THE ORGANIC VARIETY

After we've incorporated a philosophy as part of our life, we develop hope. *Hope is an inner sense of our own possibilities, derived from our personal understanding of the purpose of human life. True hope is confidence in the wisdom, direction, and guidance of the Universe. It is the understanding that the ultimate outcome of all processes in life is Goodness.* Trust is the other face of hope.

It is helpful to distinguish between true and false hope. With false hope, we place our faith in a set of beliefs, expecting a tangible outcome — security, reward, salvation, success, etc. This type of hope is false, because it leads us to impose various belief systems and personal designs on the course of the Universe. It is false because it closes us off to what truly *is* and distorts our perception of reality. Possessing true hope, on the other hand, is to be open, to know and be satisfied that we figure in the destiny of the Universe and that the Universe shares in our destiny.

ZONE THREE: ORGANIC CHANGE

The third level of striving is reached when organic change begins to take place in our being. Organic change has to do with changes in feelings and moods, and with the reconfiguration of our nervous and hormonal systems. These changes do not occur as acts of will. They take place when we have sufficiently educated the different parts of our being so that they all want to participate in the wonderful adventure that the transformational life actually is.

Organic change requires three activities, represented in the diagram by the three boxes forming a triangle at the bottom of the diagram. The activity represented by the box at the top of the triangle is that of "Clarifying the Aspirations." The activity represented by the box at the bottom left is that of "Feeling the Terrestrial Equivalent of Universal Values." The third box to the bottom right represents outer behavior: "Adjusting the Being to Accord with One's Understanding of How Universal Principles Manifest Themselves in an Earthly Setting."

The three boxes are connected in a very dynamic relationship. This results in growth, and since the three activities reinforce each other, the consequence is a continuous spiral of awareness.

Clarifying the Aspirations

The task of clarifying the aspirations involves the activity of meditation. This is the exercise of seeking to become emotionally clear on what we seek. This is what we called "generic meditation" in Chapter 6. Our aspirations can be very vague until we take time to settle on what it is that we want from life. Here we are forced to confront what it is we want out of our transformational pursuits: *Is it comfort and protection, or is it awareness and the responsibility and challenge that awareness brings?*

The type of meditation required here consists of three stages.

- First, we must select which of our spiritual aspirations we want to make clear.

- Second, we attempt to arrive at a feeling understanding toward what this aspiration implies.

- Third, we determine what adjustments we will have to make in our outer life (attitudes) and daily living (activities) to achieve compatibility with this aspiration.

The exercise of clarifying our aspirations can have practical implications in helping us to take responsibility for our vision of a better life.

An Exercise in Taking Responsibility for our Vision

A vision is a blueprint. It is an ideal, meaning that which will manifest itself when all the barriers to its expression are removed. A transformational vision is the existence we will create for ourselves if all the barriers to Self-expression fall away. Do you not have a vision? Why are some people afraid to embody their visions? Should a vision be buried in the ground, or should it be cultivated? The following exercise should help us incarnate our vision.

1. Where do you see yourself spiritually twenty years from now? How old will you be? What activities give you a sense of purpose at this age twenty years from now?

2. Where do you see yourself spiritually ten years from now? How old will you be? What relationship do you observe in the activities you now engage in and those you described in the previous question?

3. Where do you see yourself spiritually five years from now? How old will you be, and what are you doing now that has a bearing on what you hope to be doing five years from now?

4. Where do you see yourself spiritually three years from now? What are you doing that connects with what you see for yourself in the previous question?

5. Where do you see yourself spiritually one year from now? How old will you be? What will you be doing then? Does it have any bearing on something that you are planning or doing now?

6. Where are you on your spiritual journey *now*? How old are you? What plans do you have for the future? What do you mean by the future? Is the future one, two, five, ten, twenty years from now? Do you see any relationship between your future and your current activities?

7. Reflect on something you are doing now — career, hobby, lifestyle — that can be traced to a conscious decision you made in the past. Can you at this point recall when that which is now commonplace in your life was only a vision with fuzzy outlines?

8. What plans do you have at this time to find a birth-moment for your current vision?

The combination of a meditation practice and your effort to give outline and embodiment to your vision creates *sincerity* in your spiritual seeking. Sincerity separates authentic from superficial seeking.

Sincerity

Sincerity, in the sense that we use it here, consists of five aspects that go together to permeate the being with a certain resonance.

They are as follows:

1. A preparedness to take on the responsibilities of the higher level of consciousness that we are seeking;
2. Acceptance of ourselves for what we are, without blaming anyone for shortcomings we may observe in ourselves — not our spouses, parents, children, God, the devil, no one;
3. Knowledge that we are not yet in possession of that which we are seeking;
4. A willingness to acknowledge in others the qualities we are seeking in ourselves;
5. Openness and constant awareness that the object of our spiritual search may manifest itself in a manner quite contrary to our expectation.

We must always test our sincerity by questioning our motives for everything we do. Since most time our motives are hidden, even to ourselves, we must try to determine honestly the outcome that would satisfy us in every pursuit and interaction we engage in. This indirectly tells us what our motives are.

Feeling the Practical Equivalents of Universal Principles

As our level of sincerity is developed, it becomes easier for us to work on the bottom left box, which deals with "Feeling The Terrestrial Equivalent of Universal Principles." This is another stage in embodying our vision as we understand it after we have worked at clarifying our aspirations. The activity in this box deals with grounding our understanding of spiritual principles as we now grasp them.

An Exercise

1. List all the values, principles, and personality attributes you believe necessary for you to realize your spiritual aspirations. For example, you might include love, courage, patience, humility, peace, kindness, etc. The list can be as long or as short as you like. Write these qualities down on a sheet of paper.

2. Next, imagine that you are in a position to introduce these principles to a new culture, assuming that they do not speak your language. How would you need to behave in order to demonstrate these principles?
3. Run through each quality on your list carefully. Once you have familiarized yourself in this way with the practical implications of your aspirations, take time to see how they will change your life and society if you are able to give them expression in your being.

This exercise is also an aspect of meditation. *Actually, we can use meditation to rehearse a principle we want to incorporate into our being.* By rehearsing a principle in this manner, we strengthen our will. It is important that as we familiarize ourselves with a spiritual principle we do not judge and criticize ourselves for lack of it in our life. Such self-criticism just siphons away energy we need for the exercise.

I would have called this exercise "visualization," except that I feel there is too much confusion about what visualization is. What we are speaking of here is *the mobilization of our feelings to acquaint us with a desired situation.* It is the same ability we use when we find ourselves absorbed in a suspenseful book or movie. We derive excitement out of these activities because we are able to mentally transport ourselves into different situations.

As we become more enthusiastic about our spiritual possibilities, we are able to undertake activities represented by the box on the lower right. This box takes us a step further. It completes the cycle of organic striving by helping us undertake the action implied by a principle. The box deals with deep changes in our being: Here we *do* because we see the necessity of action. The attitudes mentioned in Chapter 7 are specifically suited here as a practice, because they assist one to recalibrate the being — to sculpt a new "me." Our hormonal and nerve impulses will change to correspond with the new person we are becoming. Once we have achieved this degree of change we are able to do "good" deeds without effort or any expectation of reward. Good deeds are now a natural and spontaneous expression of our beings as a result of our consciousness becoming established at a higher level. We can start by making small changes in our life by focusing on little things. A friend told me that she stopped littering. Another person stopped running red lights, and yet another started being more attentive to other people.

ZONE FOUR: IMPLICATIONS OF SPIRITUAL CONSCIOUSNESS

As we work on ourselves, there are certain spiritual developments we can watch for. We should try to see the extent to which the following are manifested more and more in our being and outlook on life.

1. To what extent is your perspective on what is "good" changing from what is advantageous to you to what is in accordance with Divine Will?
2. To what extent has your understanding of success changed from being better than others or acquiring more than others to awakening your own creativity and contributing to awakening the creativity of others?
3. To what extent has your motivation for doing spiritual work changed from wanting something to the realization that you have no real choice but to do the work for its own sake, and that there is really no viable alternative available for your energies?
4. To what extent have you stopped valuing knowledge for its own sake in favor of that knowledge that provides you with insight as to the next step you need to take on the spiritual journey?
5. To what extent are you able to see the absolute futility and uselessness of pretense and of wanting to be seen by others as other than what you actually are?
6. To what extent have you come to see and accept that every individual on this planet has an equal right to all that you value for yourself? (For example, freedom).
7. To what extent are you comfortable with your activities such that even if you knew you were to die while engaged in them you will have no incentive to change them?

Final Exercise:

1. Consider what it might feel like if all the human emotions existing right now were to be averaged out — all the pain, the joy, the disappointments, the triumphs, the sorrows, the expectations, the despair! How does God experience all of us together?
2. Consider your life as an invocation. Imagine that everything you do, say, feel, think, attracts to you certain Cosmic Energies. What sort of Cosmic Energies will you attract by the way you live your life right now, assuming you do not change anything? How will you modify the invocation of your life if you want to attract a different quality of Cosmic Energies?

GLOSSARY

CHAPTER ONE

The Transformational Impulse The deep and unarticulated need within humanity for meaningfulness.

The Evolutionary Impulse The impulse toward adaptation, which expresses itself as the need for survival, belonging, and acceptance.

Individualizing One's Being To seek out the place in the Universe that has been created with one specifically in mind.

Acknowledging the Transformational Impulse Giving the quest for meaning within oneself the cooperation of the will, mind, body, and Soul, the latter defined as the aspirations and yearnings.

Clarifying the Aspirations Contemplating the scope and dimension of what life is and what it requires of one. This requires specifying what one ought to make the objective of striving in personal life.

Value System A method of identifying, in practical terms, what the concrete or time-space effects of achieving a particular level of striving will be. It is also a set of criteria that one uses (consciously or unconsciously) to arrive at a decision to undertake or not undertake a particular action.

Biopsychic Functioning The interrelationship between desires, thoughts, hormonal states, actions, and the way these influence the organization of psychic energy.

CHAPTER TWO

Subjective Values Behavioral criteria that are determined by personal preferences and societal standards.

Universalizing One's Being Having motivation to act with a greater good in mind than personal comforts or maintaining societal norms.

Universal or Objective Values   A system wherein the values in question become more valid as the number of people who uphold them grows.

Egocentric and Ethnocentric Values   *Values that lose their validity as the number of people who adopt them grows, since they conflict with the egocentric and ethnocentric values of others.*

Objective Existence   Having one's "reason for being" validated by the act of other individuals sharing the same one.

Conscience   An awareness of the objective world of others and the ability to take their well-being into consideration when making plans for one's own welfare. Through this faculty, goals for the community become translated into personal goals and personal actions are placed in a Universal context.

Will   The capacity of an individual to voluntarily engage in actions that facilitate his or her own growth. Operationally, Will can be regarded as the drawing force of a Greater Whole in very much the same way that a cosmic body such as the sun exerts a pull on the earth or the earth on the moon.

Quality of a Question   A question has quality depending on the degree of sincerity with which it is asked and the breadth of the concerns that it embodies.

Progressive Perfection   The orientation of one's sense of identity to a larger and larger center, such that one strives for greater and greater achievements and realizations.

Shadowing   The process by which an individual functions at a level of being beyond his natural abilities. This is accomplished by conscious sacrifice. Shadowing is also known as "priming the pump."

Priming the Pump   See Shadowing.

Spiritual Consciousness   A quality of being that is sensitive to the necessity, existence, and beauty of the tendency towards wholeness in life. Implications of this tendency towards wholeness are Love and cooperativeness.

CHAPTER THREE

Defining the Transformational Impulse   (a) Getting a "feeling sense" of the Universal need that is behind the Impulse; (b) seeing each individual as a Path; (c) developing quality control procedures from which to fashion a philosophy of life.

Narcissistic Complex   This is the impulse toward sensation and runs counter to the quest for meaning in that one is unwilling to take responsibility for one's life and actions.

Symbiosis   A mutually supporting and sustaining relationship between different levels of life expression.

Path   A task of minding the milieu created by the interaction of two different levels of reality, human and spiritual.

Transformation of Consciousness as an Autonomous Process   The view that the transformation of consciousness has its own rhythm and laws and does not restrict itself to man-made systems and barriers.

Divine Milieu   The result of the intermingling of forces created by the down-reaching of our collective future which already exists and an individual's personal consciousness striving to improve itself.

CHAPTER FOUR

Personal Philosophy   A lifetime plan of action.

Trajectory   A flight path that specifies the route to be taken between a point of departure and a destination.

Relevance   The determination of the frame of reference or the context within which a system of ideas developed and whether that system can be taken out of its context and applied to another situation.

Pertinence   The precision of fit of a teaching. It is concerned with the appropriateness for oneself of a system that seems appropriate for others.

Intentionality   The extent to which it is logical to set specific objectives of human striving when these objectives may or may not be under human delegation.

Continuity   The basic meaning of experiences in the extent to which it is logical to project and extrapolate the center of one's perceptual world into the future.

Verifiability   The determination of the validity of a revelation or a given bit of information, in this case, of a spiritual nature.

Consanguinity   Literally means "of one blood," but in this context means the ability to detect equivalence between a principle one upholds and its expression in action.

Congruence   The extent to which a doctrine converges with one's personal reality.

Archetype   A symbol of a high psychic order that has not yet been subjected to conscious elaborations (as expressed by Jung).

Objectivity   The evaluation of an idea or a teaching from outside of the group or the culture that upholds it.

CHAPTER FIVE

Focusing the Transformational Impulse   Relating to transformation as a spiritual psychology.

Spiritual Psychology   A method of making conceptualizations about transformation concrete enough for the individual to use them to form aspirations and influence attitudes and actions.

Purpose in Life   Having a feeling sense of what is possible for one as an individual human being.

Spiritual Orientation   A way of securing and maintaining integration in the psyche.

Purpose in Use   A way of relating to the purpose of life in terms of a goal or set of functions, or having a certain societal role.

Purpose in Process   A sense of being fully engaged in life such that one is oriented toward the dynamics of growth rather than toward a specific goal or set of goals.

Truth   An attunement to Reality, to Wholeness.

Integration   The restoration of a sense of wholeness to the psyche from the state of fragmentation to which it is prone. The term is derived from the term "integer," which means "whole."

Self–Remembering   The act of keeping aware of a sense of the harmonious functioning of one's separate parts.

Envelopment or Immersion   A way of committing the whole being to transformation without regard for rewards, whether these be temporal or celestial.

Temporal Integration   The harmonization of the inner world of ideals and beliefs with the outer world of action.

Spatial Integration   Being open to new possibilities, being receptive. One does not spend one's energy defending fixed positions.

Horizontal Integration   The same as Temporal Integration.

Vertical Integration   The same as Spatial Integration.

Giving an Open Option to God   One refrains from placing images in the way of the Transformation Impulse, in the sense of having preconceived ideas of how it will manifest itself in the personal life.

Seeing the Transformative Journey as One Unit   One does not separate the journey into means and goals.

Acquisitive Approach to Transformation   One relates to transformation as adding to that which one already has of a worldly nature.

Eliminative Approach to Transformation One relates to transformation in terms of getting rid of that which is not of the true Self.

Asymptosis Derived from the mathematical concept, the asymptote, which defines a relationship where a curve approaches a straight line at such an angle that it gets ever closer but is unable to actually touch it. Asymptosis in spiritual life occurs when our expectations get in the way so that we can never directly realize that for which we are striving.

Innocence (As an antidote to Guilt.) A way of exploring a past indiscretion for its potential for creating new understanding of the human condition and for increasing one's commitment to transform one's being.

CHAPTER SIX

Psychology of Meditation Study of changes in perception and emotional states gained from various meditation practices.

Philosophy of Meditation The determination of what meditation seeks to put to right in an individual.

Fragmentation A condition of inability to bring all of one's various parts together to work in unison for the good of the whole being.

Generic Meditation A contemplative undertaking to discern how fragmentation could be overcome and effectiveness returned to an individual's conscious will.

Sincerity Ability to get an emotional reading on what it is that one is aspiring to become.

First Stage of Generic Meditation An effort to come to grips emotionally with the implications of one's ideals and aspirations.

Second Stage of Generic Meditation The readiness to make a commitment to carry out personal adjustments in one's life.

Third Stage of Generic Meditation Becoming master of one's own attention so that one is able to bring into manifestation in the mind and daily activities the ideals that one already holds.

Shared Perfection The engagement of practices to strengthen the linkages in an individual between various parts of the being, for example, between the mind and the body, the spirit and the mind, and the spirit and the body.

CHAPTER SEVEN

Sacred Space An emotional-mental environment that is open and receptive to all that Life has to offer.

Facilitating the Transformational Impulse   Undertaking actions that satisfy the quest for meaning in life, thereby sustaining the quest.

Humility   A personal characteristic of not being loath to share the ordinary fate of ordinary men and women.

Faith   The process of attuning oneself to the "supersensible" worlds.

CHAPTER EIGHT

Separativeness   A feeling of being alone, incomplete, and cut off from others due to a state of psychological fragmentation.

Tantra   A psycho–spiritual technique of Eastern origin that allows an individual to overcome a desire preoccupation by surrendering to it.

Apperception   A certain quality of consciousness wherein one can experience oneself experiencing.

CHAPTER NINE

Spiritual Teacher   One who embodies, in the flesh, the spiritual ideals a spiritual seeker already holds for himself.

Avatar   A spiritual teacher who embodies a Universal Principle so that individuals can see it in a concrete context.

Savior   Same as Avatar.

Savant   One who excels in a particular quality or virtue. A Spiritual Teacher in a local context as opposed to a Universal one.

Catalysts   Organic enzymes that trigger a certain process of change and dissolve to become part of the end product itself.

Distant Light   Someone who holds out a vision for humanity to reach for.

Charlatan   Someone who aspires to the role of the spiritual teacher because he or she thinks that there is glamour and prestige in this function.

CHAPTER TEN

Spiritual Experience   Any encounter that has the effect of enhancing and broadening an individual's perception of the world. It may result in a permanent transformation of the individual's life.

Psychic Experience   An experience that may involve other than ordinary means of perception. Unlike a spiritual experience, there is no *a priori* reason why a psychic experience may change an individual's life.

Intuition A higher integrative faculty of perception that manifests itself as a result of the harmonious functioning of one's being.

Chapter Eleven

Omega Point A concept used by Pierre Teilhard de Chardin to designate the culminating point of collective human evolution.

Supramental Manifestation A concept used by Sri Aurobindo to designate the next stage of evolution for human life on Earth.

The Resurrection The idea, as espoused by the early Christians, that the existence of individuals who are dead will be restored, but with a new body.

Chapter Twelve

Attenuating the Ego The lessening of the dominance of the ego in one's life affairs.

Involuntary Suffering Includes most forms of suffering that stem from an inappropriate orientation to life.

Voluntary Suffering Also known as intentional suffering (according to Gurdjieff). This occurs when one consciously chooses to undergo immediate discomforts for the sake of long-term benefits.

Developmental Suffering Suffering experienced as a result of the preparation necessary to give embodiment to a higher level of being and existence. It is a necessary part of spiritual growth.

Dispensational Suffering Suffering that is experienced as a result of being part of a group.

Karma A perspective on the operation of Divine justice that believes that an individual must meet the consequences of all actions done in the body, good or bad.

Dark Night of the Soul A certain intensity of suffering, isolation, and alienation brought about when all the support structures that aid and abet an individual's ego-centered perception of self fall away.

Death of God A stage in the transformational process where the seeker is forced to change the nature of his relationship with Existence to a more mature one. This demands that the individual withdraw all the projections that had been previously placed on God. In reality, it is not God that dies, but one's idea of God that must die before the Presence of God can be known.

Enlightenment   The other side of The Dark Night. A quality of existence free of the illusion of a separate existence from the ALL.

Unscrambled Awareness   A quality of consciousness where one is able to clearly perceive the consequences flowing from the actions that are undertaken.

Functional Karma   An advancement of the idea of karma. This concept recognizes that the difficulties one experiences may not necessarily have anything to do with past bad deeds, but that some difficulties are opportunities to invoke a higher level of Reality to share one's personal reality.

CHAPTER THIRTEEN

Tonight's Dinner Syndrome   The tendency to go back on a commitment to develop the character or change the nature due to a lack of fortitude to press on in the face of practical difficulties.

Equanimity   A quality of being that is sustained by a realization that the Universe bodes us no ill. This allows us to experience difficult situations with acceptance and patience. Such composure helps to detoxify those situations at a spiritual and psychic level.

REFERENCES

The author cites the Revised Standard Version of the Bible.

Aurobindo, Sri. "The Hour of God." Reprinted in *The Essential Aurobindo*, edited by Robert McDermott. New York: Schocken Books, 1973.

Aurobindo, Sri. *Savitri — A Legend and a Symbol*. Pondicherry, India: Sri Aurobindo Ashram Trust, 1972.

Bynner, Witter, (Translator). *The Way of Life According to Laotzu*. New York: Capricorn Books. 1962.

Dass, Ram. *Grist for the Mill*. Santa Cruz, Ca.: Unity Press, 1976.

The Fellowship for Spiritual Understanding. *The Golden Rule in Ten of the World's Great Religions*. Palos Verdes Estates, Ca., 1972.

Guillaumont, A., et al., trans. *The Gospel According to Thomas*. New York: Harper & Row, 1959.

Keyes, Ken, Jr. *The Hundredth Monkey*. Coos Bay, Or.: Vision Books, 1982.

Moody, Raymond, Jr., M.D. *Life After Life*. New York: Bantam, Books, 1976.

Needleman, Jacob. *Lost Christianity — A Journey of Rediscovery to the Center of Christian Experience*. New York: Bantam Books, 1982.

Ouspensky, P.D. *In Search of the Miraculous*. New York: Harcourt Brace Jovanovich, 1949.

Rajneesh, Bhagwan Shree. *Meditation: The Art of Ecstasy*. New York: Harper & Row, 1976.

Teilhard de Chardin, Pierre. *The Phenomenon of Man*. London: Fontana Books, 1965.

van der Post, Laurens. *Jung and the Story of Our Time*. New York: Pantheon Books, 1975.